MINECRAFT
in the Classroom

Ideas, inspiration, and student projects for teachers

Colin Gallagher, Editor

with Shane Asselstine · Dan Bloom · André Chercka · Adam Clark
Stephen Elford · David Lee · John Miller · Eric Walker · James York

Peachpit
Press

Minecraft in the Classroom
Ideas, inspiration, and student projects for teachers

Shane Asselstine, Dan Bloom, André Chercka, Adam Clarke, Stephen Elford, Colin Gallagher, David Lee, John Miller, Eric Walker, and James York

Peachpit Press

Find us on the web at: www.peachpit.com

To report errors, please send a note to errata@peachpit.com

Peachpit Press is a division of Pearson Education

Editors: Clifford Colby and Robyn Thomas
Production editor: Tracey Croom
Compositor: Maureen Forys
Indexer: Valerie Haynes Perry
Copyeditor: Scout Festa
Cover design: Mimi Heft
Interior design: Mimi Heft

ISBN 13: 978-0-133-85801-3
ISBN 10:   0-133-85801-4

9 8 7 6 5 4 3 2 1

Printed and bound in the United States of America

Dedication

I dedicate this book to my family back home in Ireland. We may be far away, but you have always supported my decisions in life. I also dedicate this book to my wife, Sharyn, and my other family in Cleveland, Ohio. Thanks for putting up with me, everyone!

My friends in Singapore, in Ireland, and spread around the world. Thanks for making the journey fun. Block by block.

Acknowledgments

Thank you to all the teachers who agreed to take part in this book. I know it's not the easiest of things to do, but you were all up for the challenge. Thank you also to all the teachers and students I've interviewed in my Minechat series on YouTube—you are truly inspiring.

Thanks must go out to the school administrators around the world (including my own) who put their trust in their teachers in implementing things like Minecraft in their schools.

Thanks to all my teaching colleagues who have put up with me and had faith in all the Minecraft projects we undertook.

Thanks to Rob and Joel and my wife, Sharyn, for taking the time to look over some chapters. Finally, thanks to Robyn and Cliff for keeping me on track throughout the making of this book.

Contents

Introduction

When I first installed and started playing Minecraft (alpha release) back in 2009, I didn't know I was stumbling into something that was about to explode with popularity worldwide. Minecraft looked way different back then. There were no potions, no wolves, and no ender dragons, and there was no redstone. As I fashioned a rudimentary pickaxe out of wood and tunneled into a nearby mountain for the night, I was amazed at how engaged I was. For a game with graphics out of the '80s, the gameplay and engagement was something that I had not experienced before. As strange noises emerged out of the darkness of a cloudy full moon sky, I was thoroughly immersed in surviving the night and making it through to craft another day. Something was different about this game.

With each version of Minecraft that has been released, its creator, Markus Persson (Notch), has added and tweaked things. As Markus handed the reins to his trusty sidekick Jens "Jeb" Bergensten, Minecraft evolved; more and more people had their interest piqued, and more so when Creative mode was introduced in 2011. Creative mode removed all obstacles in the way of immediate creativity and building; there was now no need to spend time crafting materials.

The first time I became aware of Minecraft being used in education was when I stumbled upon some videos uploaded to YouTube by an American elementary school teacher, Joel Levin. I remember being very excited by what he was doing and how he had planned and crafted his Minecraft world to slowly introduce students to the nuances of playing Minecraft. He was steering them away from the aspects of Minecraft that had little educational value and corraling them into the areas where he saw massive educational potential. I also remember being very excited by how he was recording and uploading screencasts of his students' experiences in Minecraft as they happened.

My adventure with Minecraft in my school started in 2012, when I organized an afterschool club for third through fifth grade students. I used an outside host to set up a creative world in which my students could unleash their creativity and imagination. With the afterschool club a roaring success, the third-grade teachers and I decided to integrate Minecraft into the third grade curriculum the following school year. The year after that, we integrated Minecraft into the first and second grade curriculum, but this time using MinecraftEdu.

Minecraft in the Classroom

Today it seems as though everyone is talking about Minecraft in education. When teachers see what students are doing, they quickly see how they can apply it in their classrooms, although some are unsure how to get started. With that in mind, I was determined to make sure teachers around the world could grasp what teachers are doing. For this they would need to see the Minecraft world and hear what teachers had to say about how they were using Minecraft in education. I started the Minechat series on YouTube to accomplish just that. I hope this book will build upon the Minechat series, provide a convenient repository of examples of using Minecraft in education, and provide a framework for beginning the adventure of teaching and learning with Minecraft.

Minecraft has changed the way people look at a wide range of cultural norms—from education to urban planning. It has been turning heads since 2009, and in recent years it has been turning educators' heads with its sandbox-like environment and its ability to be modified to suit curricula. Children and adults alike revel in the freedom Minecraft allows in planning, creating, and collaborating in many ways.

Minecraft doesn't seem to be disappearing any time soon, so let's start leveraging its appeal and engagement in teaching and learning.

Who Is This Book for?

This book is designed to help teachers get started with Minecraft, and to be inspired by what other teachers around the world are doing with Minecraft. This book is also for parents and families to be informed on how Minecraft is used in an educational context.

Who Am I?

My name is Colin Gallagher. I'm originally from Ireland, but I've been traveling the world working in the educational technology field since 2003. I've been working at ISS International School in Singapore since 2011, and in 2013 I also started working for Michigan State University as an online instructor for their Master's in Educational Technology program. Along the way I've presented on many aspects of educational technology at conferences around Asia, including TEDx in Bangkok. I've become an Apple Distinguished Educator and a Google Certified Teacher and connected with many like-minded teachers around the world on Twitter and Google+.

I've played computer games all my life, and I find it a fun and engaging hobby. Education and gaming became intertwined when Minecraft started being used in teaching. For me that's a perfect marriage.

I started wondering how teachers were becoming informed on Minecraft in education. The perfect way to know what people are doing is to see the world and hear the teacher, so I came up with the Minechat series on YouTube: http://goo.gl/peS1Qg. In it, I interview teachers over Skype while recording our tour around the world. Twenty-six episodes later and I'm still looking for more teachers to add to the channel to keep teachers inspired and informed about Minecraft in education.

I also wanted a place that teachers could join and just type up questions or add links to interesting Minecraft-related articles. For this, I created a Google+ Community: http://goo.gl/bBvRjW.

As of this writing, we have over 2000 members and counting.

With this book I'm hoping that teachers have an additional resource they can look at to garner ideas or to know who to contact with their questions about Minecraft in education.

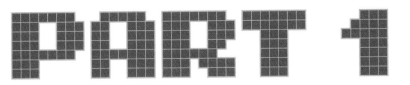

PART 1

Minecraft in Education:
The Basics

What Is Minecraft?

The beauty of Minecraft is that it can be a very different experience for each person who plays it. If you ask non-videogame-playing adults what Minecraft is, they might say that it is like digital Lego. If you ask videogame-playing adults, they might say that Minecraft is a first-person sandbox game that centers on placing and removing blocks, with different game modes and the option to play single-player or multiplayer. If you ask children what Minecraft is, their answer will no doubt be very different. And more entertaining!

"Minecraft Is..."

With every new batch of students with whom I use Minecraft, I like to ask them to finish the sentence "Minecraft is..." and record their answers on video. It's a great way to document the wide spectrum of reactions students have to the game. Here are some examples of what some third grade students say. Minecraft is:

- "a great way to use your imagination to build things"
- "a very fun game that lets you build your own houses and be creative"

- "a good way to express how you feel and build it"
- "a game of creativity"
- "a computer game that is made out of blocks"
- "a really fun game to play, and you have to be intelligent to use it"
- "cool and awesome because you can build a lot of stuff"

Now of course a lot of students bring their experiences from using Minecraft at home into their explanations and will mention wolves, zombies, and skeletons, but at the core of it all is every player's unique perspective on Minecraft.

The Basics

I could write an entire book on what Minecraft is and how it works, but let's just take a look at the fundamental aspects of Minecraft and what you need to know as a teacher. If you can't tell by the name, at the heart of Minecraft are mining and crafting (**Figure 1.1**). But it's not as simple as that, because mining and crafting don't have to take place in a certain game mode. And to make things even more complicated for teachers, there are also MinecraftEdu (a special modded version of Minecraft for education) and Minecraft Personal Edition (for tablets and phones). We'll touch on these versions of Minecraft in Chapters 2 and 5, respectively.

To start with, let's take a look at Minecraft's game modes.

Figure 1.1 Where it all begins when you load regular Minecraft.

Survival Mode

Survival mode is what most of your students will play at home. It's good to know about this mode so you can differentiate between what you're doing at school and what they are doing at home (**Figure 1.2**).

Figure 1.2
Here I'm in the Create New World screen. The name of the world will be "Ireland!" and I'll be playing in Survival mode.

In this mode you have to craft, and you have to mine to create tools so you can gather different types of blocks. There are animals you can kill to get their meaty goodness. You have health and you have hunger (**Figure 1.3**), so you can die. There are monsters that will hurt you and explode beside you. Although it doesn't sound like fun, it is, and children love this mode because it is a rewarding, challenging adventure.

Figure 1.3
I'm losing lots of health to an unfriendly skeleton in Survival mode. This will happen—a lot.

I have not used Survival mode with students, but I have heard of teachers using it to teach food production and the food chain, which I can see being very useful.

Creative Mode

In Creative mode, you have everything at your disposal for building things. There is no need to mine or craft, and those pesky monsters can't harm you. Basically, you are free to be creative—and fly (**Figure 1.4**). This is the mode most teachers use to create their worlds, because distractions are minimal and there's no need to spend time on finding resources and crafting.

Figure 1.4
Get a bird's-eye view in Creative mode.

Hardcore Mode

This is almost the same as Survival mode, but when you die, you lose everything you have collected, and the game is over. I've never used this with students.

Seeds and More

On the Create New World screen for each game mode is a More World Options button, which opens a screen with even more options for configuring your world (**Figure 1.5**). Here you can enter a seed, which designates coordinates so you can spawn to a place in the world with a specific set of features. Seeds are shared by people all over the Internet.

You can turn on and off the option of having random structures like villages and dungeons. If you don't want these as distractions, you might want to turn off this option. You can also change the world type to suit your needs. For example, you might want to change it to a flat world if you don't want mountains and ravines to get in the way of your students' creations. Allowing cheats is off by default, and there's a reason for that: Cheats allow players to type in commands to change aspects of the world, such as the game mode. Finally, you can have bonus chests off or on. If this is on, a chest appears at the spawn point, filled with essentials to help you through your first night in Minecraft.

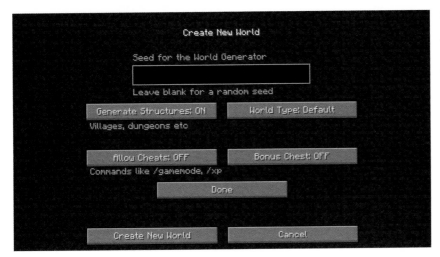

Figure 1.5. More options to tweak your Minecraft world await you.

Let's talk a little about how you can play with other people.

Single-player, Multiplayer, and Realms

In single-player you are on your own—maybe that's what you want. But even in single-player, you can open your world to people on your local area network (LAN)—this is usually the case in schools. When you create a single-player world and then press Esc on your keyboard, you can choose to open your world to LAN (**Figure 1.6**).

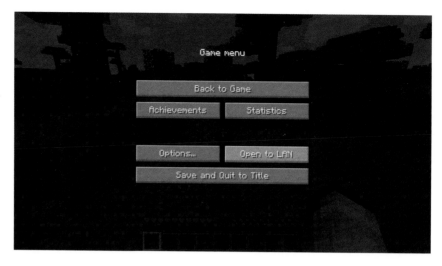

Figure 1.6
If you click the
Open to LAN
button, people
on your network
will see your
world when they
go to the Mul-
tiplayer screen.

In multiplayer, you can join other Minecraft worlds either by joining one on your local network or by entering an IP address of a world anywhere in the (regular) outside world.

Minecraft has recently added its own way of allowing people to play with friends; they call it *realms*. It's not free and there are limitations: it costs $13 a month (or less if you sign up for longer) and allows only 20 people to join your realm, with only 10 people able to play on the realm at the same time. It may suit some small classes that want to get together 24/7 for a month-long project, because it does away with messy technical setups.

In Game

In my experience, teachers need to have a basic knowledge of two main aspects of Minecraft: movement and building. This allows you to solve small student problems such as getting stuck or not being able to stop flying around. You'll also find that students readily help each other before any teacher intervention can occur. The shiest student in the classrooom can become a vocal savior in times of need.

Movement

Movement in Minecraft is set, by default, to a set of keys and mouse movements. The illustrations in this section are taken from a presentation I showed first grade students when introducing Minecraft. I purposefully left out the button for crouch/descend (the Shift button) in **Figure 1.7** because I wanted to keep it simple (and I wasn't introducing flying yet). This also allowed me to see if the question of how to crouch arose during class, initiating discussion.

Figure 1.7
The essential keys for moving around.

When I was showing the instructions for placing and removing blocks, it was also necessary to show students the role of the mouse (**Figure 1.8**).

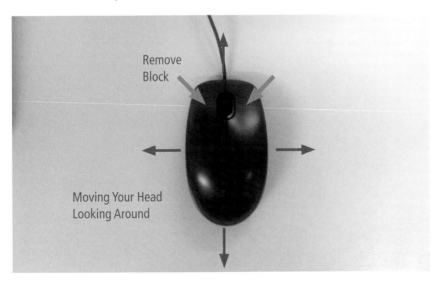

Figure 1.8
The fundamental mouse movements.

The keyboard and mouse working together allow you to do whatever you want to do in Minecraft (**Figure 1.9**).

Figure 1.9
A little bit of
math helps here.

Moving
Building

Building

As you saw in Figure 1.8, the left and right mouse buttons are for removing and placing blocks, but the big question is, Where do you get those blocks? Whether you are playing in Survival or Creative mode, you access your inventory in the same way: by pressing E (**Figure 1.10**). Of course, in Creative mode your inventory is stocked to the brim with goodies, while in Survival mode you have to work for a well-stocked inventory (**Figure 1.11**).

Figure 1.10
When introduc-
ing this aspect of
Minecraft to stu-
dents and teach-
ers, I make sure
to use keywords
such as *drag*
and *left-click*.

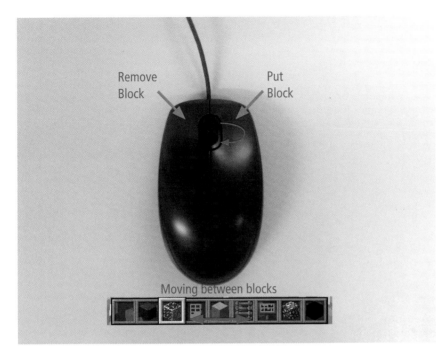

One other key that I introduce to students is the message key (T), with which students can type onscreen messages (**Figure 1.12**). I encourage this when a class is getting a little too boisterous with conversations—this will happen, so expect it.

Figure 1.12
Messaging gets younger students used to communicating with typed text. Should they use the best English they can when communicating with others? Yes.

If you've practiced the basic movement and building keys, then you are well on your way to using Minecraft with your students. As I say to my fellow teachers, "You don't have to play Minecraft every day to successfully use it in education—but it helps!"

Note   *You can change the keys associated with certain actions by going into Minecraft's settings. You may find that some students use different keys at home and so change them on a classroom computer as well. This can be confusing if the next student is used to the default keys!*

Working with MinecraftEdu

When I first started using Minecraft in my school there was no MinecraftEdu, so I used regular Minecraft (or as it's usually called, *vanilla* Minecraft). It was tricky and tested my patience to set up a server with the various mods and plug-ins. I was fortunate that a company was offering free Minecraft hosting for schools at that point, which made life a lot easier.

As a teacher you really just want to get a Minecraft world up and running so that students can be in one world together. Some teachers use MinecraftEdu, and some use Minecraft. Which one is right for you? To help you make up your mind, in this chapter I run through setting up a Minecraft world in MinecraftEdu, and in the next chapter I cover vanilla Minecraft.

Getting MinecraftEdu

MinecraftEdu is a modded version of Minecraft created to make it easier for teachers and students to set up and run the type of Minecraft world you want in your school with a minimum of hassle. TeacherGaming, the company behind MinecraftEdu, is officially supported by Mojang, which just adds more credibility to an already excellent tool for teachers.

MinecraftEdu makes purchasing Minecraft accounts easier and cheaper for teachers. The fact that you are purchasing the Minecraft accounts from MinecraftEdu does not mean you have to use MinecraftEdu; you can use those accounts on vanilla Minecraft if you wish.

Because I want to make this process as clear as possible, let's get the costs and registration process out of the way (it's what you'll do first as a teacher) before we delve into the added advantages that Minecraft-Edu brings to the classroom.

Comparing Costs and Registering Accounts

MinecraftEdu offers discounted Minecraft accounts for teachers at $18 each, or $14 when purchasing 25 or more accounts, compared to $26.95 for a vanilla Minecraft account. You do not need to purchase the MinecraftEdu mod if you just want to purchase the discounted accounts, but the MinecraftEdu mod costs $41. This tool allows you to set up a Minecraft server easily in minutes and gives you access to a wide range of useful teacher tools. I highly recommend purchasing it.

When you purchase the accounts you get Minecraft gift codes that you enter into minecraft.net after you register an account (**Figure 2.1**). Each code is linked to an account and enables you to log in to Minecraft with the account's email address.

Registering Account Emails

When you are registering multiple accounts on minecraft.net, which emails do you use for the Minecraft accounts? I created an email address under my school domain (we are using Google Apps) and used the old Gmail trick of adding +1, +2, and so on after the email user name; for example, minecraftuser+1@myschool.com. This allows me to control all Minecraft accounts in one email inbox.

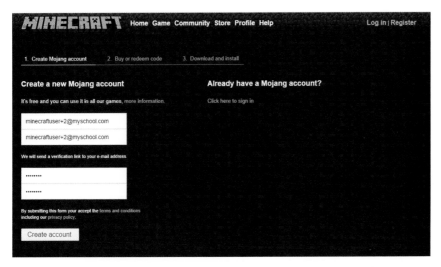

Figure 2.1
First you enter a
working email
address and
password.

After verifying your email address, you will be directed to your Mojang
account page, where you can redeem your gift code (**Figure 2.2**).

Figure 2.2
This is where
you redeem the
gift code that
MinecraftEdu
sends you.

You can download Minecraft for free; it's the user account that costs
money. Without the user account you can't play Minecraft. The user
accounts are what MinecraftEdu helps you with, and they make the process of purchasing multiple accounts a lot easier. Once you redeem the
code, you will be able to log in to Minecraft with the the email address
and password you used to register.

If you purchase the MinecraftEdu mod, you can log in to MinecraftEdu's website and download it at any time (**Figure 2.3**).

Figure 2.3
MinecraftEdu
recently revamped
their website.
Looking good.

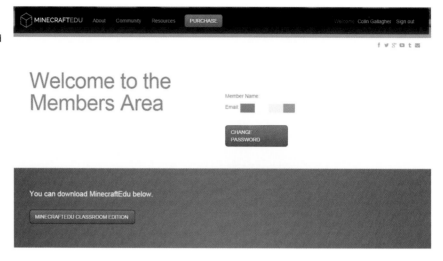

Minecraft Server and Client Installation

You need to run the MinecraftEdu mod on a computer that will act as your Minecraft server. I chose an iMac in our media lab. It's not terribly powerful—it has only 4 GB of RAM, but it runs the server without a problem.

You will see when you download the file that it is named something like "minecraftedu classroom." This is not just the server creation file but also the file you will install on your student computers so they can access the MinecraftEdu server you create. When you run the Minecraft classroom file the first time, you go through a simple wizard to install it on your computer. The "server"option of the file is not selected by default, so you will need to select it to create a server. You should leave this unselected when you install MinecraftEdu on your student computers (**Figure 2.4**).

You'll also want to have the wizard install an icon on your desktop, so be sure that the Place MinecraftEdu Shortcut on Your Desktop option is selected.

Server Setup

After running the MinecraftEdu wizard with the server and desktop icon options selected on the computer you are using as your server, you will see the MinecraftEdu icon on your desktop. To set up your Minecraft server, use the following general steps:

1. Double-click the desktop icon to launch MinecraftEdu.
2. Click the Start MinecraftEdu Server Launcher button (**Figure 2.5**).

Figure 2.5
On student com-
puters if you did
not select the
server option
during installa-
tion, they will
not see the Start
MinecraftEdu
Server Launcher
button.

When you run the server launcher for the first time you will be prompted for a teacher password (**Figure 2.6**).

Figure 2.6
Teachers have
access to more
tools in-game
than students do.

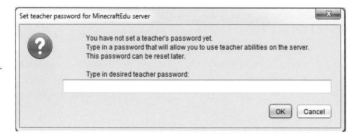

3. Enter a password and click OK.

   You'll see the main server creation menu (**Figure 2.7**) with many options, including:

   ▪ **Start Server with Tutorial World.** I use this with first grade students because it is basically a big obstacle course that gets students used to moving and building.

- **Create New World.** More than likely, you'll choose this option when starting. This option gives you the freedom to create the world you want.
- **Select a Saved World.** You will use this once you have created a world and want students to go back into it.
- **MinecraftEdu World Library.** You can choose existing worlds that have been created by teachers (some that are in this very book!). The teachers make them available for you to change as you need to. Clicking this will bring you to the world library on minecraftedu.com, from which you can download the map you like and have it appear in your own library. Very easy.
- **Load Last Played World.** Click this to play the last world that was loaded.

We want to start a world from scratch.

Figure 2.7
Where do you want to go today?

4. Click the Create New World button. Again, you have choices to make—down to what you want your students to do in your world (**Figure 2.8**).

   - **Create a random world.** This will create a random geographic world for you. You can't predict what it will look like.
   - **Generate a World from a Seed.** Seeds can be entered here in MinecraftEdu.
   - **Generate a Completely Flat World.** This is a good choice if you want your students to create without distraction.
   - **Generate Structures.** This will place random structures (like villages and dungeons) in your world.
   - **Generate Animals.** This will place random animals, such as pigs, sheep, and cows, around your world .

Figure 2.8
What do you
want your
Minecraft world
to look like?

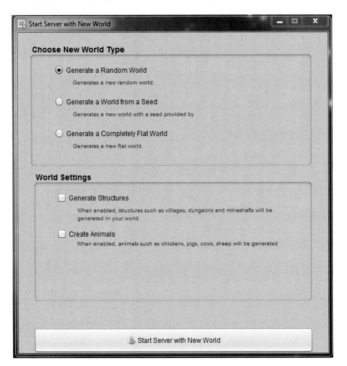

5. Select the Generate a Completely Flat Word option.

   Now I have the option to use a pre-made world type.

6. Select Classic Flat from the Pre-made World Types drop-down list (**Figure 2.9**).

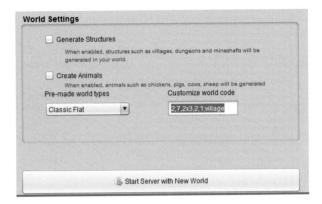

Figure 2.9
Additional
options become
available when
you generate a
flat-world map.

7. Edit the code in the Customize World Code field if required.

   The Customize World Code field on the right references the block codes in Minecraft. You can search for block codes at http://minecraft-ids.grahamedgecombe.com/.

   The default code in Figure 2.9 (2;7.2x3,2;1;village) will generate a map with one bedrock layer, two dirt layers, one grass layer, one stone layer, and villages sprinkled around.

8. Once the settings are in order, click the Start Server with New World button.

   You have successfully created your new world.

Configuring More Options

After you successfully create your new world, you can control everything in it without actually being in the game. The IP address of the server on which you installed the MinecraftEdu server and created your world displays at the top of the screen. This is the IP address that you'll enter in the Multiplayer area of each student computer.

At the top of the screen are some buttons. The most important one is the Save Map button (**Figure 2.10**). The first time you save your map, you must enter a name and click the Save Map button. Anytime you save after the first time, you'll be prompted if you want to overwrite your map. You might have instances when you want to keep an older version of the map, so just enter a new name. For example, I created one map for three classes. I set up the map once and saved it three times under a different name. This saved a lot of time.

Note
Depending on your school network settings, you might need to talk with your technical staff about IP addresses and ask them if turning off the computer that has the Minecraft server installed will change its IP address upon restart. This happened to me, and I had to re-enter the IP address on each student computer. Lesson learned.

Another important button is Stop Server, which will shut down the server. The Advanced Settings button, which I never use, gives you the option to type in advanced commands. For example, you could type /defaultgamemode creative, and it would change the game type to Creative. I talk more about these commands in the next chapter.

Here's a quick rundown on the menu options available on the left of the server screen (**Figure 2.11**):

- **Server Information.** This gives you the IP address, as well as helpful links to MinecraftEdu articles about how to play on and run the server.

- **World Information.** This is a brief overview of how your server is set up. You can also set welcome messages and daily messages for players here.

- **World Settings.** Here you can change the game mode and difficulty level, and you can turn off numerous effects and items. This will look different according to what you wish to do in your world. As you mouse over each option, an explanation displays (**Figure 2.12**).

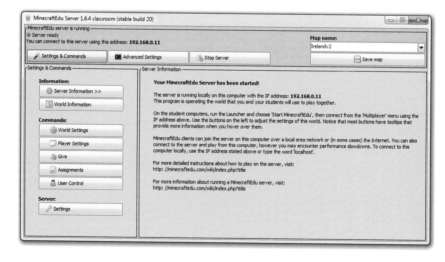

- **Player Settings.** Here you can control what your students can do, along with freezing them, teleporting them, and muting them from messaging each other (**Figure 2.13**).

- **Give.** If you're not set to Creative mode, you can give blocks to students.

- **Assignments.** If you want your students to perform specific tasks, you can set them here. No need for paper anymore.

- **User Control.** This gives students the ability to password-protect their aliases.

Figure 2.12
Pay close attention to the game modes and difficulties, because they will radically change the players' experiences. I normally choose Creative and Peaceful.

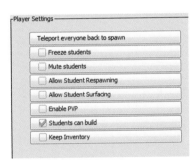

Figure 2.13
Students Can Build is an option that I select all the time.

Getting Students into Your Minecraft World

MinecraftEdu must be installed on every student computer. You need to run the MinecraftEdu classroom file you downloaded on every student computer, individually. I usually push the file out using Remote Desktop (you may need to ask your technical staff), or I put the file on a USB drive. I don't usually select the Minecraft Server Launcher option; the icon will be on the desktop. Enter the IP address into the Multiplayer area when you start up MinecraftEdu. I usually input the IP address myself before a project so we don't waste time in class. Students will use the following general steps:

1. Double-click the MinecraftEdu desktop icon.

   When loading MinecraftEdu, students will see a few differences from their regular Minecraft experiences.

2. Click the Start MinecraftEdu button from the launcher menu.

3. Select an option for how you want to log in from the Login Mode drop-down menu: a Mojang Account, MinecraftEdu (I use this with younger students who aren't the best at typing yet), or a Mine-craftEdu Hosting Account (this is a new option, as MinecraftEdu is currently developing MinecraftEdu hosting services) (**Figures 2.14** and **2.15**).

4. Enter the Mojang account email and password. (These are the ones that I created as minecraftuser+1@myschool.com, minecraftuser+2@myschool.com, and so on.) Click the Login button.

Figure 2.14
Choosing MinecrafEdu is a little tricky to remember for younger students, but they quickly get used to it.

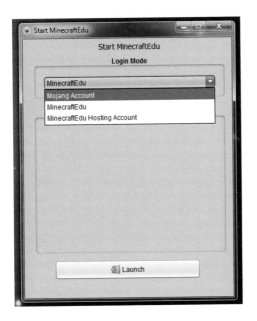

Figure 2.15
You may want to
print out email
addresses and
passwords for
each student.

5. Enter your name, click the appropriate button for your gender, and click Continue (**Figure 2.16**).

Figure 2.16
Students love
this part!

If students have played Minecraft before, they will see a more familiar area (**Figure 2.17**).

Figure 2.17
The only dif-
ference on the
menu screen
is the title:
MinecraftEdu
as opposed to
Minecraft.

6. Click Multiplayer.

7. Click the server displayed in the center of the screen (**Figure 2.18**), then click Join Server.

Figure 2.18
Save time by
entering the
IP address for
the students
before they get
to this stage.

8. Choose a skin by clicking the right and left arrows to scroll through the skin options. Click Connect, and you are in (**Figure 2.19**)!

This is also the area where teachers can choose I Am a Teacher, enter a password, and do some cool teacher things in game. We'll look at this next.

Figure 2.19
Sometimes students take a while to figure out what they want to look like on that particular day.

Accessing the Teacher Menu

If you log in as a teacher you get access to a whole bunch of in-game tools that help you organize and manage your world. By pressing P on your keyboard, you gain access to the Minecraft Teacher Menu (**Figure 2.20**).

Useful tool tips pop up when you hover over any option, but let's go through each menu to see what you can do as a teacher.

- **Personal Menu.** This is what you see when you go into the teacher menu. You can turn on Spectator mode to make yourself invisible, and you can turn on Creative mode for you only (if you are not in a Creative mode world). You can also spawn yourself back to the ground if you are stuck in a big cave somewhere, and you can spawn back to spawn, which is the area at which you came into the game. There is also a slider to change your movement speed.

- **World Settings**. These are settings that affect the whole world. You can also change these from your server settings, as you saw earlier in this chapter (**Figure 2.21**).

Figure 2.20
A myriad of
teacher tools
await.

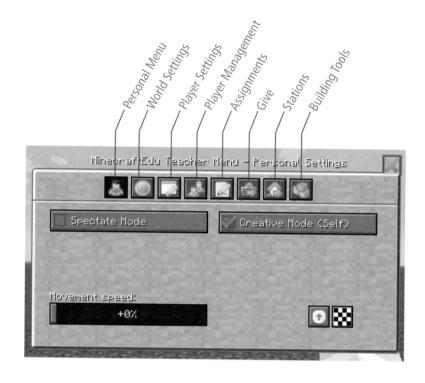

Personal Menu
World Settings
Player Settings
Player Management
Assignments
Give
Stations
Building Tools

MinecraftEdu Teacher Menu — Personal Settings

Spectate Mode

✓ Creative Mode (Self)

Movement speed:

+0%

Figure 2.21
If you suddenly
want to allow
TNT, this is the
menu you want.

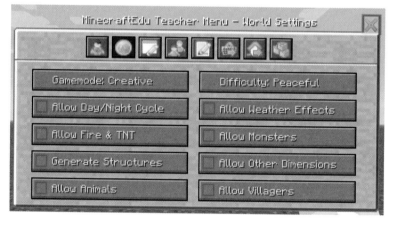

MinecraftEdu Teacher Menu — World Settings

Gamemode: Creative

Difficulty: Peaceful

Allow Day/Night Cycle

Allow Weather Effects

Allow Fire & TNT

Allow Monsters

Generate Structures

Allow Other Dimensions

Allow Animals

Allow Villagers

- **Player Settings**. These settings affect what players can do (**Figure 2.22**).

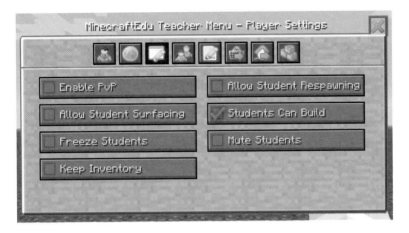

Figure 2.22
Things getting a little crazy? You can freeze all your students here.

- **Player Management**. Here you can search for specific players (or all) to be teleported to you, to be teleported to them, to be frozen, to enable/disable text messaging, to be allowed in Build mode (more on this later), or to be changed to different game modes (**Figure 2.23**).

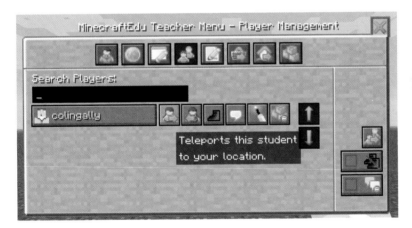

Figure 2.23
Having full control over every student is what makes Minecraft-Edu so powerful for teachers.

Assignments. Write assignments for students here. A pop-up will appear for each student. They press M on their keyboard to see the assignment, and when it's complete they put a check mark beside it (**Figure 2.24**).

Figure 2.24
Giving in-game assignments can be very useful to keep students on track.

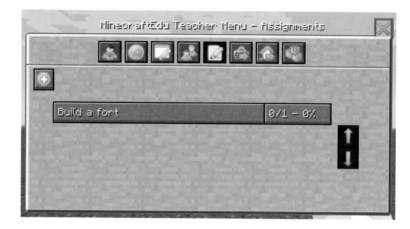

Give. If you're not in Creative mode, you may need to give some blocks to some or all of your students. You can do that in this menu (**Figure 2.25**).

Figure 2.25
Some blocks of dirt coming colingally's way!

- **Stations**. If there are teleport stations set up in your world, you can go directly to them by clicking them here (**Figure 2.26**).

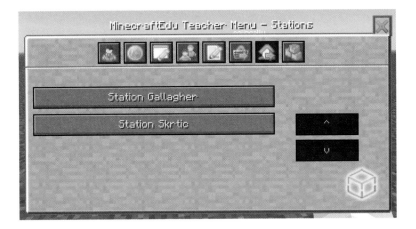

Figure 2.26
If only teleportation existed in the real world.

- **Building Tools**. This menu is very important to teachers who want to build structures and areas for students and want to do it in the most effective way possible (**Figure 2.27**). Turning on Building mode allows you to build way off in the distance (**Figure 2.28**) and to go through solid blocks, among other things. Another powerful tool is the Fill/Clear tool, which allows you to fill in and clear out vast areas in a matter of clicks (**Figures 2.29** and **2.30**). Other options here allow you to undo the last placements of blocks, the last fills, and the last blocks destroyed. You can also set the number of blocks that will be placed or destroyed in a column.

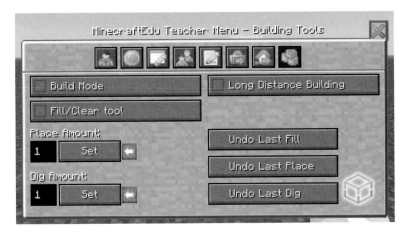

Figure 2.27
Turning on these options will allow you to build more effectively and efficiently.

Figure 2.28
Building mode is very handy for building large structures quickly. If you can see the black square on the ground, you can build from where you are. This is a lot farther than you can usually build.

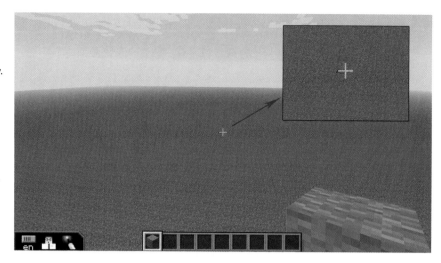

Figure 2.29
I've clicked once to set one corner of an area and now will click again to fill that area with the purple wool block.

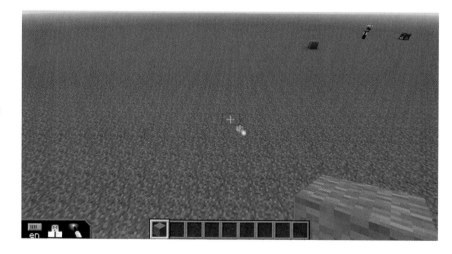

Figure 2.30
And voilà, just
what I wanted.

Using MinecraftEdu Blocks

One last thing to know about MinecraftEdu is the additional MinecraftEdu blocks you have access to as a teacher (**Figure 2.31**). The blocks are:

- **Block Inspector.** This gives you information on a block as you hover over it. At the time of this writing, this block is under development to add more functionality.

- **Build Disallow Block.** Place this block where you don't want students to build. Even if students have the right to build in the world, placing these will disallow students from building or digging above them. For example, these blocks would come in handy if you wanted to create a welcome building that you didn't want destroyed or added to.

- **Build Allow Block.** Place this block where you want students to build. For example, if you want to create a world where building is allowed only in certain areas, you could disable student building but place the Build Allow blocks in the areas in which you want students to build.

- **Information Block.** This is a block where you write pages of information. You will read in the forthcoming chapters multiple uses for this block. It's a very important block for teachers to use.

Note

Note: If you're not in Creative mode, you will have to turn it on from your teacher menu (press P on your keyboard).

- **Information Sign.** Use this block to indicate that there is an information block to read.

- **Border Block.** Use this block to prevent students from going to certain areas or to just have them not wander off too far. I have used these to keep energetic second grade students within an area in which we can keep them focused on the work at hand.

- **Spawn Block.** This is the block where everyone will enter the game and respawn if they meet a sticky ending. If a teacher places many spawn blocks, the respawn/spawn will be set to the last spawn block placed. Students can't destroy spawn blocks.

- **Foundation Block.** This block measures the distance between foundation blocks.

- **Teleport Block.** Place these blocks to create a network of teleportation areas. By default, the teleportation blocks the students can teleport to are invisible to students, so you have to turn on the visibility in each teleportation block if you want them to be usable. If you want only teachers to use these teleportation blocks, then keep them invisible.

- **Home Block.** This is a relatively new block that allows you to set your personal home coordinates.

Figure 2.31
Some additional blocks that will come in handy as a teacher in MinecraftEdu.

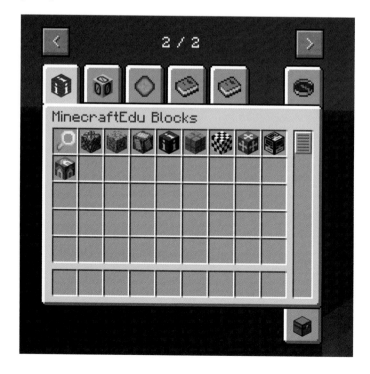

Making Your World Accessible from Outside Your School

The process of setting up your server and installing the MinecraftEdu launchers on your student computers will make your Minecraft world accessible only from within your local network at school. There are ways to get your server accessible from outside your school, but they differ so much, depending on your network setup, that I can't possibly go into it and leave room for other chapters!

The technical support staff at your school can help you open up your server if you so wish. It involves opening ports on the school firewall, so you may have to do some convincing about the educational advantages of this. You may also wish to get in touch with the teachers in this book who have successfully opened their servers to the world or have arranged with outside hosting companies to host their MinecraftEdu server.

A Quick Word on Mods

When you open your MinecraftEdu launcher, you'll see a Mods menu (**Figures 2.32** and **2.33**). Mods are modifications that people have created that you can download, and they can radically change how Minecraft looks and acts.

Figure 2.32
By clicking the Mods button I can quickly access mods that radically change my world.

Figure 2.33
I have some mods loaded already in my world, but I can also click Switch to Online Mods and see what else there is to use.

A very popular mod to use in the educational setting is Custom NPCs (**Figure 2.34**), which can add more interactive characters to your world. You can set up conversation trees and develop quests with this useful mod. When you start looking at mods, you'll really begin to see what is attainable in Minecraft.

Figure 2.34
NPC stands for non-playable character.

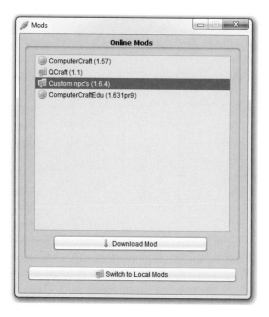

As you can see, MinecraftEdu provides a lot of options that cater to making educational spaces within Minecraft easier for you, the teacher. Getting started with MinecraftEdu is but one step along a long journey in using Minecraft in education. I am sure the guys at TeacherGaming will be enhancing it constantly to make the experience even more fulfilling. Hopefully, you now have an idea of what to expect when using MinecraftEdu for the first time.

Working with Regular Minecraft

There are a myriad of options available for you to set up a Minecraft server if you don't want to use MinecraftEdu. But as this book goes to press, one of the major players in creating your own server, CraftBukkit, has been subject to a Digital Millennium Copyright Act (DMCA) take-down and is no longer available for download. Other server-creation software platforms are looking precarious too, with Spigot also the subject of a DMCA take-down.

Taking this into account, we can't consider third-party software an option for setting up a server. Instead, I'll explain how to use the official Minecraft server software to set up your own Minecraft server. For updates on the status of the controversial third-party platforms, see my Minecraft in Education Google+ community, at http://tinyurl.com/glpusmc.

Installing the Minecraft Server

The following instructions are for installing the Minecraft server on a Windows 7 computer. Other operating systems are a little more complicated. You can read more about those methods at http://tinyurl.com/otherosmc.

1. Go to the official Minecraft site at http://tinyurl.com/mcoffserver.

2. Download the latest version of the Minecraft server software (at the time of this writing, it is version 1.8).

3. Create a folder called MinecraftServer (**Figure 3.1**).

Figure 3.1
Place the server installation file in its own Mine-craftServer folder.

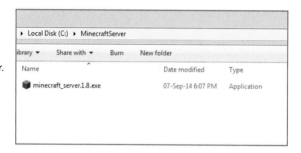

4. Place the downloaded Minecraft server installation file in the new folder.

   Make sure to put it into its own folder, because it will make files and subfolders in the folder where you are installing it.

5. Double-click the downloaded file to run it.

   A command console appears, and a number of different files generate in the MinecraftServer folder (**Figure 3.2**).

6. In the command console, type **stop** and press Enter to stop the server.

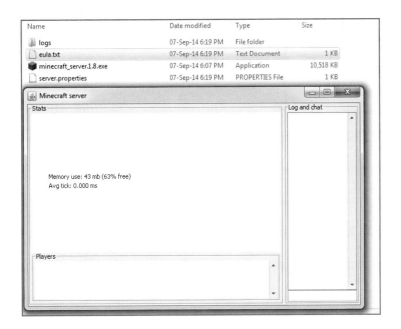

Figure 3.2
It's all looking
a little bare at
the moment.

You want to stop the server because you have something to do first
before getting started with your Minecraft world (**Figure 3.3**).

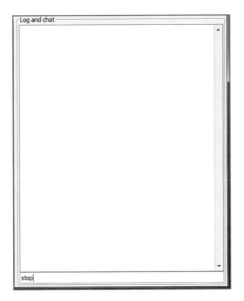

Figure 3.3
Typing stop and
pressing Enter on
your keyboard
stops the server.

Mojang has recently taken great strides in making sure Minecraft users are not doing things with Minecraft that they shouldn't be doing. To this effect, before your Minecraft server can be used, you need to agree to Mojang's EULA (end user license agreement). Following are the major points of the EULA.

You must not:

- Give copies of the game to anyone else.

- Make commercial use of anything Mojang has made.

- Try to make money from anything Mojang has made.

- Let other people access anything Mojang has made in a way that is unfair or unreasonable.

All points are very reasonable, and you must agree before continuing.

7. Edit the eula.txt file in the MinecraftServer folder (**Figure 3.4**) and change the word `false` to `true`.

Figure 3.4
Agree with
the EULA
wholeheartedly.

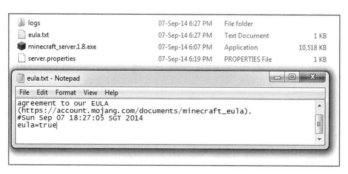

8. Save the edited eula.txt file.

9. Run the minecraft_server.1.8.exe file again. Now the full server installation completes (**Figure 3.5**).

Figure 3.5
Now you can
start configuring
your world by
editing these files.

Now what you need to do is find out the IP address of your computer so other computers on your network can access your world.

10. Hold down ⊞+R to open the Run command box.

11. Enter **cmd** and click OK (**Figure 3.6**).

    The command console appears.

12. Type **ipconfig** in the command console (**Figure 3.7**) and press Enter.

    The IP address displays (**Figure 3.8**). This is what players on your network will use to access your Minecraft server.

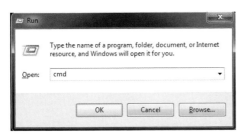

Figure 3.6
Enter cmd to display the command console.

Figure 3.7
Enter **ipconfig** in the command console to get the IP address of your computer.

> **Note**
> *Anytime you need to make changes to the files in the MinecraftServer folder, it's a good idea to stop the server with the* stop *command in the server command console.*

Figure 3.8
You can see that
the IP address of
my computer is
192.168.1.102

```
C:\Windows\system32\cmd.exe

Windows IP Configuration

Ethernet adapter Local Area Connection:

    Connection-specific DNS Suffix  . :
    Link-local IPv6 Address . . . . . : fe80::3d48:1b09:d2b0:10ef%11
    IPv4 Address. . . . . . . . . . . : 192.168.1.102
    Subnet Mask . . . . . . . . . . . : 255.255.255.0
    Default Gateway . . . . . . . . . : 192.168.1.1

Tunnel adapter Teredo Tunneling Pseudo-Interface:

    Connection-specific DNS Suffix  . :
    IPv6 Address. . . . . . . . . . . : 2001:0:9d38:6abd:88:10f:3f57:fe99
    Link-local IPv6 Address . . . . . : fe80::88:10f:3f57:fe99%12
    Default Gateway . . . . . . . . . : ::

Tunnel adapter isatap.{BA88A3DE-0F4B-4EB9-88A9-769E6E6BCF28}:

    Media State . . . . . . . . . . . : Media disconnected
    Connection-specific DNS Suffix  . :

C:\Users\Colin>
```

It may look a little daunting, but all you need to look for is "IPv4 Address" in the lines that appear in the command console.

Editing Minecraft Server Files

Once you know the IP address of your server, you need to enter it in the server.properties file in your MinecraftServer folder. I use a program called Notepad++ to open these types of files. Right-click the server.properties file, and choose Edit with Notepad++ (**Figure 3.9**).

Figure 3.9
Notepad++ is
free. Download
it from http://
tinyurl.com/
npadplus.

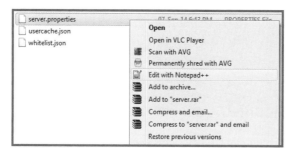

1. Open the server.properties file.

   You'll see a long list of options you can change, but right now you only need line 17.

2. Enter the IP address, and save the file (**Figure 3.10**).

```
 1   #Minecraft server properties
 2   #Sun Sep 07 18:43:21 SGT 2014
 3   generator-settings=
 4   op-permission-level=4
 5   allow-nether=true
 6   resource-pack-hash=
 7   level-name=world
 8   enable-query=false
 9   allow-flight=false
10   announce-player-achievements=true
11   server-port=25565
12   max-world-size=29999984
13   level-type=DEFAULT
14   enable-rcon=false
15   level-seed=
16   force-gamemode=false
17   server-ip=192.168.1.102
18   network-compression-threshold=256
19   max-build-height=256
20   spawn-npcs=true
21   white-list=false
22   spawn-animals=true
23   hardcore=false
24   snooper-enabled=true
25   online-mode=true
26   resource-pack=
27   pvp=true
28   difficulty=1
29   enable-command-block=false
30   gamemode=0
31   player-idle-timeout=0
32   max-players=20
33   max-tick-time=60000
34   spawn-monsters=true
35   generate-structures=true
36   view-distance=10
37   motd=A Minecraft Server
```

Figure 3.10
Once the
IP address is
entered and the
server is on, play-
ers should be
able to access the
Minecraft world.

3. Double-click the minecraft_server.1.8.exe file. The server will run.

4. Try to access the world on another computer on your network (**Figure 3.11**).

Because it's a Minecraft 1.8 server, the other players must be running Minecraft 1.8 on their computer; if they aren't, they can easily change it in their profile.

Figure 3.11
It worked! A player named colingally is now in my world.

The server.properties File

There are a lot more settings you can change in the server.properties file to make changes in your Minecraft world.

Let's take a look at the most important ones for configuring your server settings.

- level-type=DEFAULT

  You can change this to FLAT (a flat world), LARGEBIOMES (like DEFAULT but bigger areas), AMPLIFIED (world is generated to higher limits), or CUSTOMIZED (you have created a world in single-player and you are wanting to use that—more on how to do this later).

- force-gamemode=false

  If you change this to true, the player will be forced to play whatever game mode (see the next page) you set in your world; if it stays at false, the player will stay in the same mode they were last at in your world. For example, if you started a server on Survival but then changed to Creative after a few days and this setting is still on false, the players will stay in Survival.

- `max-build-height=256`

  If you don't want your students going crazy and building structures way too high, then set this to a lower value. The number value equals the number of blocks high that people can build in your world.

- `spawn-npcs=true`

  Do you want villagers wandering around your world? Change to `false` if not.

- `white-list=false`

  A *white list* contains the users who are allowed in your world. We'll talk about how to populate your white list later. If your world is open to the public and this setting is `false`, then anyone can join, which is not always good.

- `spawn-animals=true`

  If this is set to `true`, you will have lots of animals running around by default.

- `resource-pack=`

  Have you been on a server where all the blocks look a little different? That may have been a resource pack. You can add a direct link here, and it will prompt users to use that resource pack when entering your world.

- `pvp=true`

  PVP (player versus player) means fighting against other players. Turn this to `false` to stop players from hurting each other!

- `difficulty=1`

  0=peaceful, 1=easy, 2=normal, 3=hard. With a setting of 1, 2, or 3, you can take damage from mobs. With a setting of 0, nothing can harm you.

- `gamemode=0`

  0=Survival, 1=Creative, 2=Adventure, 3=Spectator. We mentioned Survival and Creative modes in a previous chapter. Adventure mode is a bit different in that you must use a specific tool to interact with certain blocks, like only allowing a pickaxe to break stone. Spectator mode allows for flying around the world without interacting with blocks or players.

- `max-players=20`

  You may need to change this to suit your class size. More players use more resources on your server computer, so you may want to keep an eye on how the world acts with different numbers of players.

- `spawn-monsters=true`

  This is just like the animals setting. Do you really want monsters?

- `generate-structures=true`

  Do you want villages and dungeons to be generated?

- `motd=A Minecraft Server`

  Change this to your very own welcome message to your students.

Note
If your server is running at the time you edit this file or any files in your server folder, you will need to stop and start your server again for changes to occur.

As you can see, the server.properties file is a very important file to look into, or you won't be able to manage your world well at all.

white-list.json File

In this file, you can enter the names of the users who will be allowed in your world. It works hand in hand with the `white-list=true` setting in the server.properties file. Anyone not in the white-list.txt file will be booted out upon trying to enter your Minecraft world. This is a good way to keep things under control. I have had older siblings coming into our world when I first started out due to a white list not being properly set up.

ops.json File

An op, or a moderator, is a player in your world who can keep control of things in-game by typing server commands in the text box. For example, an op (colingally) can warp himself to another player (MrGallagher) by typing `/warp colingally MrGallagher`. There are many commands available to ops that help in moderating a world.

In the ops.json file, you can type in the names of the ops of your world, whether they are teachers or students.

logs Folder

In the logs folder, you can see what has been going on in your world while you've been away. For example, you can see who logged on, what they said, and when they logged off (**Figure 3.12**).

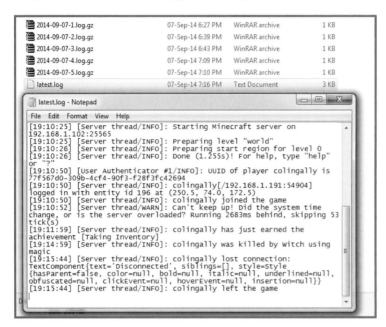

Figure 3.12 colingally did not have a good time during this session.

world folder

You can paste an already-made world into this folder. If you have a single-player map that you want to be the world that your students see, simply copy and paste all the files and folders in your single-player world into this folder.

The method for finding your single-player worlds differs from operating system to operating system, but here is how to do so on a Windows 7 computer:

1. Click the Windows start button and type **%appdata%**.

2. Click the Roaming folder, then open the .minecraft folder. Your single-player worlds are in the saves folder.

Note
Stop your server, delete all the files that may be in your world folder already, and then do the copying and pasting.

Minecraft Server Command Console

When your server is running, you'll always have the command console up. In it, you can enter some quick commands that change the world immediately.

Note *At the time of this writing, the Minecraft Server 1.8 console does not show the commands that you type or any confirmation that the commands were successful. You must check the latest.log file in the logs folder to see if your command was successful. I'm sure that this is a bug that will be fixed.*

Here are some good commands to know.

- help

  By typing help you will get all the commands you can use in the command console.

- defaultgamemode

  Instead of going into the server.properties file, you can change the game mode here (**Figure 3.13**) by typing: `defaultgamemode creative`

Figure 3.13
I have now changed the world to Creative mode.

```
[20:22:46] [Server thread/INFO]: The world's default game mode is now
Creative Mode
```

- time

  If it's getting too dark to build, you can control time (**Figure 3.14**). Set it to dawn by typing: `time set 0`

Figure 3.14
I now have a full day of daytime ahead of me.

```
[20:32:13] [Server thread/INFO]: Set the time to 0
```

- weather

  If you are tired of constantly sunny days, change it up a bit. For some thunderstorms (**Figure 3.15**), type: `weather thunder`

Figure 3.15
All changes to weather occur in real time in your world.

```
[20:33:49] [Server thread/INFO]: Changing to rain and thunder
```

- op

  Instead of changing the ops.json file, you can op a player from the console (**Figure 3.16**), just type: `op colingally`

  ```
  [20:35:03] [Server thread/INFO]: Opped colingally
  ```

Figure 3.16
colingally now
has more power
in this Mine-
craft world.

There are many other commands, but with the files, folders, and commands I've covered, I think you'll be good to go.

Minecraft in Education—Why?

You may have had to answer some questions from school administrators, parents, and other teachers as to why Minecraft is so important to implement in your school. Normally, just looking at teachers' work online (especially in my Minechat series!) is enough to prove the benefits, but sometimes a clear set of reasons comforts people more.

If you ask teachers around the world why they use Minecraft, they might come up with a wide array of answers. I've listed my reasons in this chapter, but I'm sure I'll add to the list as teachers find more incredible ways to use Minecraft in their teaching.

Collaboration

Working with other people is probably the most challenging aspect of school (and life). Teamwork activities happen regularly during the year in my school, and they involve students trying to learn a lot of very tough collaborative skills, such as negotiating, listening, following directions, and accepting criticism. I think that we, as adults, also struggle with these things at times.

In Minecraft, there is huge potential for developing these collaborative skills. I've talked with dozens of teachers about their Minecraft projects, and they explained that usually students work together to complete tasks. If they are not working together, they are usually in the same world trying to ignore distractions and avoid conflicts. Minecraft is, in essence, a social game. It begs to be played with other players. In an educational setting, students can work on collaborative skills in Minecraft when planning, building, and presenting a project as a group.

When students work as a group in Minecraft, it is vital that they work effectively. There's something interesting about Minecraft: Often, at least initally, working together effectively does not happen. I think the freedom is too much for some students, or they have not adjusted to using Minecraft in an educational setting. Conversations, guidance, and advice between group members and between groups and teachers can help develop the collaborative skills needed for effective group work.

Creativity

Every generation has something that enables young people to let their creativity run wild. For my generation, that was probably Legos. Someone might argue that Legos were many generations' outlet for creativity. I admit, though, that growing up in Ireland I had a lot of outside play and exploration, which also unleashed my creative side. A great big world awaits our students' exploration, too, and not just in Minecraft.

Minecraft has enabled young people from kindergarten to college to start creating. Minecraft has inspired people to re-create everything from spacecrafts to entire cities. Minecraft has inspired people to create stories, poems, paintings, and animations. Creating things in Minecraft inspires creativity in other ways. For example, a very popular project to have students underake is to re-create their school. As this is being done, students are naturally compelled to think about what their ideal school looks like and what changes they would make to their current school.

You could look at an empty Minecraft world as a blank canvas awaiting a player's unique creativity. The lines between art, design, architecture, and urban planning are becoming thinner in Minecraft. Without knowing it, children are sowing the seeds of their passions in life and of what may be in store for them in their professional careers.

Differentiation

We learn very early on as teachers that not every student is the same; they do not learn the same way, and they might not be able to convey their learning in the same way. I have had many students whose first language was not English or who found it difficult to write their final assessments because of learning disabilities. Differentiating for students generally means giving them different avenues to explore content, understand content, process that content, and create content.

Technology has always been a major factor in providing students those different avenues: video and audio platforms as instructional tools, animations and digital comic strips as tools to create content, and Google Apps as a way to organize learning.

Minecraft has been used to differentiate in a number of ways. You will see a lot of examples in this book about how it could work with the wide array of different learners in your class. You can create immersive worlds as a visual, interactive, and informational field trip so students can attain more than just words on a page. Students can create worlds to present their learning on a subject matter that they might not have been able to reproduce on paper. Some fifth grade students in my school last year created hydroelectric dams and solar panels within Minecraft as a way to demonstrate their learning on energy. The student that created the dam was not a native English speaker, but from looking at the intricate working parts on the dam, I could instantly see what he had learned.

As differentiation is such a widely discussed and important aspect of education, it is worth noting that Minecraft might not be the best tool for every aspect of differentiating for a student. We cannot dismiss it, though, because it's another powerful tool you can use to help students.

Digital Citizenship

Digital citizenship goes hand in hand with collaboration and can be a vitally important lesson in managing a digital life for our students. Minecraft is a digital world and you do not see your collaborators face to face, which can lead to some interesting scenarios for our students. Usually it is hard for a student to communicate online with others; it is not something they have had to do before. They may have viewed YouTube videos and seen the horrendous comments and believed that "anything goes" online.

When griefing (damaging other people's stuff) occurs in Minecraft, it can be an amazing moment for students to learn not just about digital citizenship but about property ownership, responsibility, and respect. You may find that the sweetest student in your class does some mean things once behind a computer screen. What students type in Minecraft when they think nobody is monitoring is another learning moment that deals with their perception of what they think is right and wrong to type online and how nothing online is temporary—there's always a record somewhere.

A major spinoff from Minecraft is the amazing YouTube culture it has created—people who want to show off their Minecraft work make a YouTube channel. A lot of students in my school have Minecraft YouTube channels. Along with YouTube, sadly, comes a negative part of digital life: the criticisms, the trolling, and the dislikes. For students and adults alike, it is very difficult to take the anonymous and sometimes downright nasty feedback. These can be very hard but powerful learning moments for students. Parents need to be aware of their students' online activities, so I always conduct a yearly session with parents to educate them about how to manage their children's digital lives.

Engagement

In this day and age, engaging students is difficult. Teachers have to stay current with modern teaching and best practices just to stay afloat in the classroom. Engagement is tricky because not every student is alike and they don't all have the same interests.

I have been using Minecraft in school for four years, and I have not come across a student who did not like it and was not immediately engaged. That amounts to zero in about 250 students. That is one amazing statistic. Students are engaged with Minecraft, and it's because of the reasons listed in this chapter: it's a creative space, it's fun, and it's relevant to them.

Fun

Yes, fun is good. But is fun enough? Sometimes, but it's best when fun is accompanied by engagement and a well-planned project. Students find Minecraft fun because they get to be creative and because it's technology—and they like both those things because that's where they are in their lives. They live with technology daily, and for children creativity is a major source of pride and a feeling of accomplishment. Adults like Minecraft because we can be creative again, and that's fun.

Independence

The controls in Minecraft are not difficult to master. My first grade students had it down after a few sessions. When it comes to independence in the real world, younger students are still a little bit restricted, but inside Minecraft they can take control and do what they feel like doing. Students love showing off their work in any form, but from start to finish in Minecraft they are truly in charge of their creativities.

Leadership

In every school around the world is a student who knows Minecraft inside out. These students are often the second (or sometimes first) teachers of Minecraft in the class. The leadership these students take on is a powerful and meaningul experience for them, and most times they are students you would not pick out as natural leaders. Minecraft gives opportunities to students to lead, organize, and mentor their classmates, which leads to more confidence in themselves.

Relevance

Look around you in the restaurant at lunch; look around you on the bus or train to or from work. Most people are staring at devices instead of books or newspapers. Now this may be a good thing or a bad thing, but I'm not going to get into that. My point is that students were born into *this* world. Of course they should know about (paper) books, and books should be a part of their lives, but students see their parents with a technological device rather than a book every day.

Our students are in the middle of this world and living this life with us. Technology is relevant. Video games are relevant. This is what it's going to be like for a very long time, and if we don't make this a part of their educational life too then we are doing them a disservice.

PART 2

Minecraft Classroom Projects

Teaching with Minecraft Pocket Edition

I interviewed David in May 2014 in his regular Minecraft world, where he had set up activities for his students. He was showcasing activities he had already undertaken. It was David's work with Minecraft PE (Pocket Edition) that really got me interested in it, as there are a number of differences between Minecraft PE and vanilla Minecraft that affect how projects need to be planned and executed.

Project Summary

The fourth grade "Boundaries and Volcanos" unit focuses on one of the disciplinary core ideas of the Next Generation Science Standards (NGSS). This core idea states that "most earthquakes and volcanoes occur in bands that are often along the boundaries between continents and oceans."

Based on this idea, students create their own virtual 3D boundaries and volcanoes to explain and describe these large-scale system interactions (formative assessment). In this performance assessment, students take on the role of museum curators who are faced with the problem of low museum attendance among young people. To resolve this problem, students create an online exhibit that young people are more inclined to visit. The driving question of the unit is "How do we as museum curators create

David Lee
I have a master's degree in educational technology and am an elementary technology teacher and educational technology specialist at Korea International School (KIS) in Seongnam, Korea. I provide students with project-based learning activities that focus on authentic tasks. The technology skills and concepts students acquire are crucial to their development as 21st-century learners.

I offer educators professional development sessions and classroom facilitation to implement tech-enhanced practices into their instruction and curricula. I've been a conference presenter at the KORCOS 2012 and 2014 conferences and the 2013 Google in Education South Korea Summit.

davidleeedtech.org

a digital Boundaries and Volcanoes exhibit for students to visit online?" Ultimately, students video-record themselves explaining their large-scale system exhibits and publish their video online to share with peers, parents, and teachers (summative assessment). This authentic challenge compels students to create a meaningful and practical product that is connected with the real world.

The teaching method for this science unit is project-based learning (PBL), a method that allows students to investigate and find solutions to complex challenges. According to the Buck Institute for Education (BIE), the essential elements of PBL are:

- Significant content
- Student-led inquiry
- Development of 21st-century competencies (critical thinking, problem solving, collaboration, communication, creativity, and innovation)
- Activities centered on the driving question
- The need to know
- Student choice
- The revision and critiquing process

Throughout the unit of inquiry, students focus on the driving question to foster their investigation of the large-scale system interactions and create the solution to their authentic problem.

Project Goals

The focal goal of this unit is to have students understand, demonstrate, and explain how tectonic plates interact with one another to form geological features. Minecraft Pocket Edition is the ideal educational tool for this unit because the game enables students to demonstrate understanding of academic concepts in a way that was not possible previously. This open-world game is ideal for the culminating project because it equips students with unlimited cubed resources to freely create their plate boundaries and volcanoes. Students interact with their creations and experience them in a 3D simulation world.

Another goal of the unit is to develop students' 21st-century skills and knowledge. According to the International Society for Technology in

Education (ISTE), successful student learning involving technology incorporates six components:

- Creativity and innovation
- Communication and collaboration
- Research and information fluency
- Critical thinking, problem solving, and decision making
- Digital citizenship
- Technology operations and concepts

These crucial skills and knowledge allow students to learn effectively in this digital age, work on higher-order thinking skills, and help them accomplish real-world, authentic tasks.

Learning Objectives

In this unit, students reach project goals by:

- Identifying different types of plate boundaries
- Creating digital models of a plate boundary (transform, convergent, or divergent)
- Creating a digital model of a volcano
- Labeling the different components of their plate boundaries and volcano models
- Recording video of themselves explaining in detail what transpires in their plate boundaries and how a volcano is formed
- Practicing safe and responsible use of educational technologies

To assist students in completing these learning objectives, the teacher calls to mind the driving question, "How do we as museum curators create a digital Boundaries and Volcanoes exhibit for students to visit online?" and the essential questions throughout the unit. Here are the essential questions, which are open-ended and foster inquiry and understanding:

- What generates plate boundary activity?
- How do the activities in plate boundaries affect the earth?
- Why do volcanoes appear on Earth? How are plate boundaries involved in this process?
- Where should a person live if he or she does not want to encounter earthquakes?

Organizing the Project

It is important to note the time frame of the project, considering both preparation and implementation time.

- Teacher preparation time: Two to five hours
  - 30 minutes for finding boundaries and volcano resources
  - 30 minutes for finding a Minecraft PE seed
  - 3 hours for creating example boundaries and volcano models. If time is limited, the teacher can show the example images that are provided in this chapter (Figures 5.5 through 5.7).
  - 1 hour for creating a video explaining the models
- Project duration: Four to five weeks
- Student classroom time spent on Minecraft PE project: Approximately 400 to 500 minutes (50 minutes per class session)
  - 3 class sessions for research
  - 3–4 class sessions for creating the models
  - 1–2 class session for creating the video
  - 1 class session for students to share videos
- Other tools: Minecraft PE, tablet computer, video recording app, movie-creating app, YouTube

Outside Minecraft

Before the start of the Minecraft project, students thoroughly research the different types of plate boundaries and the volcanoes that are formed (**Figure 5.1**). This inquiry process involves rigorous student-led questioning and using relevant online resources provided by the teacher. The driving question generates student motivation to obtain the crucial knowledge and skills required for the completion of the project. It is recommended that students be given a formative assessment to monitor the progress of their learning before entering the Minecraft phase of the unit. For example, the teacher can have students complete exit slips (prompts given at the end of a session for students to reflect on and express what was learned), learning logs, or graphic organizers to identify whether or not they are meeting learning outcomes.

Inside Minecraft

I chose Minecraft PE, the mobile version of Minecraft, for this project because of our upper elementary's one-to-one iPad program. The program requires that every third to fifth grade student use an iPad in the classroom for academic purposes. Students simply install the Minecraft PE app onto their iPads to get started on their challenge. The PE version, available for both iOS and Android devices, is especially great in the classroom setting because it allows students to be mobile during Minecraft group activities, enabling and enhancing student-to-student interaction, communication, and collaboration.

Minecraft PE vs. Minecraft PC

Minecraft PE is similar to the Minecraft PC version in that it includes Survival and Creative modes, infinite worlds, biomes, mobs, and villages. The key difference between the two versions is the crafting element of the game. In Minecraft PE, players can craft an item by using the Minecraft Advanced Touch Technology Interface System (MATTIS) instead of the 2x2 and 3x3 grids. In this system, players craft an item by collecting essential materials, then tapping on the item and its button (**Figure 5.2**).

Figure 5.2
Minecraft
inventory user
interface.

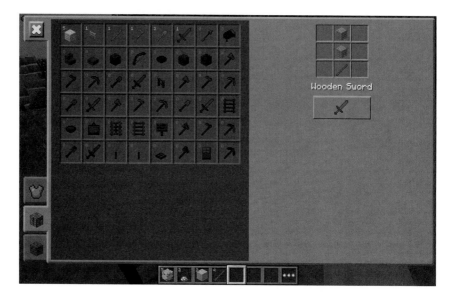

As of the most recent version, 0.9.0, notable features and items missing from Minecraft PE are various mobs (horses and dragons), the ability to modify the appearance of objects (items, blocks, animals, and so on), the absence of Hardcore mode, and text commands for advanced functions. However, it is important to note that with every update, Minecraft PE is becoming more like the PC version.

Version 0.9.0 includes the following updates:

- Infinite worlds
- New biomes: mesas, jungles, swamps, and extreme hills
- Abandoned mineshafts and villages
- Interaction buttons to manipulate animals: Tame button to tame a wolf (**Figure 5.3**)
- Caves
- New blocks and items: granite, diorite, emerald block, monster eggs, new flowers, and so on
- New mobs: slimes, endermen, mooshrooms, silverfish, and wolves

- New world feature generations: lake, double plants, ground bushes, fancy oaks, jungle tree, and so on
- Numerous bug fixes

For the complete update list, visit the Mojang website at https://mojang .com/2014/06/pocket-edition-0-9-0-snapshot-biggest-update-ever/.

Figure 5.3
Interaction button: Tame.

Finding a Seed

Before introducing the project to the students, the teacher must find a seed that is appropriate to the project's goals. According to MinecraftSeeds.co, a seed is a specific number that generates a particular Minecraft world. If students type in a specific seed number when creating a local game, they will all generate the exact world. The teacher needs to explore different worlds to find one that contains half of a hill and an area near it that is big enough for a boundary structure. Instead of creating their volcanoes from scratch, students can use this hill to create their volcano model, providing them more time to complete the unit's learning objectives. After finding the desired world, the teacher will identify the seed number by using the Edit button on the Play screen and then share it with the students (**Figure 5.4**). I also recommend that the teacher create a visual guide that directs the students to the specified hill (**Figure 5.5**).

Figure 5.4
In the Play
screen, tap the
Edit button to
see the world's
seed number.

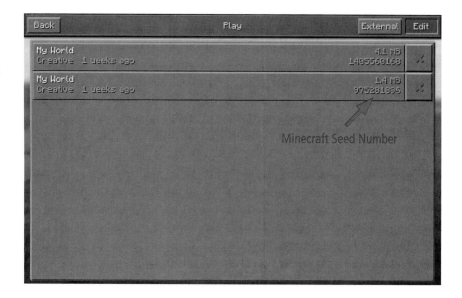

Figure 5.5
Create a visual
guide to direct
students to the
volcano hill and
area for their
boundaries.

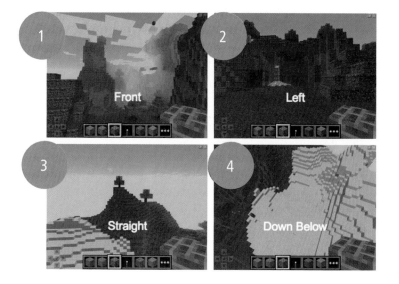

Creating Boundary and Volcano Examples

For the first year of this project's implementation, the teacher will need to create example exhibits of the large-scale systems to guide students in their own creations. The examples should include one volcano exhibit and three boundary exhibits (convergent, divergent, and transform boundary). Every major component of each large-scale system should be correctly labeled (**Figures 5.6** through **5.8**). Additionally, a video example of the teacher comprehensively explaining the different exhibits should be recorded for the students to view. Presenting these examples to students helps them better understand the project objectives and gives them a better idea of what they will be assessed on. The students will use the examples to develop new and improved ways of creating the systems. Additionally, this process will help the teacher become better acquainted with the game, learning about Minecraft PE's gameplay and the capabilities of each block and item. The knowledge gained from this experience will help the teacher better facilitate students during the project.

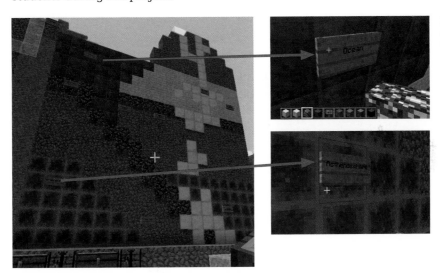

Figure 5.6
Convergent
boundary model.

Figure 5.7
Transform bound-
ary model.

Figure 5.8
Volcano bound-
ary model.

Getting Started

Prior to the project, there are some preparations that the teacher and students need to make, both inside and outside Minecraft Pocket Edition. Outside Minecraft PE, students are to conduct research on volcanoes and the different types of plate boundaries. The teacher needs to provide students with relevant and valuable resources to assist them in their research. Inside Minecraft PE, the teacher needs to find a Minecraft seed appropriate for the project, construct sample volcano and plate boundaries models in the game, and finally instruct the students on how to generate their world with a specific seed.

Introducing Students to PE

The first class session consists of a short introduction to Minecraft PE. This introduction is a review of the unit's objectives, an overview of the game, and a discussion on the similarities and differences between the PE version and the PC version of Minecraft. Many students will add a lot to the discussion because of their extensive experience in playing both versions. In the next session, the teacher should discuss what rules should exist when using Minecraft PE in the classroom. The teacher should start with a list of essential rules and then have students add their own recommendations to the list. Permitting students to participate in the process allows them to take ownership of the rules, motivating them to follow protocol, and play the game more critically. Here are some essential rules of Minecraft PE:

- No violence
- Respect the space and property of others

Here are some additional rules that prevent problems and disagreements:

- Respectfully ask peers to exit your premises without any violence or impolite comments.
- Do not enter your classmates' worlds without their permission.
- Turn off local server multiplayer when completing a project on your own so that no one can enter and destroy your work.
- Turn off local server multiplayer after all your group members have entered your world so that no one can enter and destroy your group's work.

You can determine your own consequences for students who break the rules, but I recommend a strict zero-tolerance policy. Any student who is found griefing, committing any act of ingame violence, or destroying another classmate's work will not be allowed to complete the project with Minecraft PE. Instead, they will need to complete the project using another medium, such as a diorama. With this policy, students are apprehensive about committing any inappropriate behaviors, because they prefer using Minecraft for the project rather than traditional classroom tools. A zero-tolerance policy can help manage the excitement of students who have great affection for the game and also create an atmosphere focused on safe and healthy learning. The teacher should emphasize that using Minecraft PE in the classroom is a privilege and not a right. It is a great tool to demonstrate mastery of the project's goals, but there are other educational options that can be used to accomplish this. Teachers have the right to revoke the privilege if students violate any of the essential rules.

Setting Up Worlds

The teacher guides the students in setting up their Minecraft PE worlds. The teacher models each step while projecting the steps onto a projection screen for all the students to see. The students are given time to complete each of the steps, while the teacher walks around to give assistance and monitor student progress. Here are the steps that the students will take in setting up their worlds:

1. Replace the default name (Steve) with your first initial, last name, and class in the Options screen.

2. After tapping the New button in the Play screen, change the name of the world in the Create New World screen.

3. Tap the Advanced button, enter the seed number that was chosen for the project, choose the Creative game mode, and then tap the Create World button.

    The game mode depends on the unit's goals. For example, if the unit's goals are to have students understand economic concepts, then Survival mode would be chosen because the resources are limited.

4. After generating the world, go to the Options screen and turn off Local Server Multiplayer.

5. Look at the visual guide (Figure 5.4) to find the hill where you will create your volcano exhibit.

The process is different if students plan to work in groups. If this is the case, one student (student A) from the group will create a world with Local Server Multiplayer turned on. The rest of the group will not need to create their own worlds, but instead will join student A's world from the Play screen. After everyone in the group has entered the world, student A will go to the Options screen and turn off Local Server Multiplayer so that no one outside the group can enter. I recommend creating groups of two to four students. Players will be disconnected if there are too many players in one world.

Guided Gameplay Practice

In another session, the teacher provides a brief overview of the game's controls and gameplay. The overview includes instruction on how to:

- Move, jump, swim, and fly with the D-pad (thumb-operating controller at the lower-left corner)
- Place blocks by tapping a specific location, and destroy blocks by tapping and holding down on them
- Add, swap, and remove items from the hot bar (the bottom bar that contains seven slots)
- Find specific items and blocks in the inventory screen
- Use the chat button in the lower-right corner of the screen to communicate in text with other players
- Change game controls, graphics, and sound settings in the Options screen

The rest of the session is allocated for students to practice building any structure they wish with the items and blocks in the inventory. The teacher can designate a few students who have extensive experience playing Minecraft PE as "master builders" and have them help their peers when assistance is needed.

Completing the Tasks

This stage of the unit is the formative assessment, in which students create their boundary and volcano exhibits. It should take the students two to four sessions to complete their exhibits, but the amount of time really depends on the students' mastery of the content and their past experience with Minecraft PE. Every session starts with a review of the project's learning objectives and a reminder of the consequences students will face if they are found griefing, committing violent acts, or disrespecting the property of others.

Before the students start their project, the teacher will provide example exhibits (Figures 5.6 through 5.8) and scoring rubrics (**Tables 5.1** through **5.4**) to help students better understand what is expected of them in the challenge. The examples and rubrics will help students monitor the quality of their work, and determine if more research is needed or if any changes to their exhibits need to take place. The four exhibits must contain all the crucial components of the large-scale systems, as well as identify each component with a correctly labeled sign. The rubric also includes the criterion "creativity and innovation." This criterion focuses on the new improvements, the originality of the models, and the models' usefulness to the targeted audience.

Table 5.1
Convergent Boundary Model Rubric

CRITERION	4	3	2	1
Required Elements	The model contains six or more elements of a convergent boundary. The model may include the following elements: lithosphere, asthenosphere, magma, oceanic crust, continental crust, volcanic arc, trench, and convection currents (elements may vary depending on the type of convergent boundary).	The model contains only five elements of a convergent boundary.	The model contains only four elements of a convergent boundary.	The model contains less than four elements of a convergent boundary.
Element Labeling	All elements are correctly labeled with proper vocabulary and no spelling errors.	Most elements are correctly labeled with proper vocabulary and no spelling errors.	Some elements are correctly labeled with proper vocabulary and few spelling errors.	Very few elements are correctly labeled with proper vocabulary and few spelling errors.
Creativity/ Innovation	The model was constructed and presented in an original and unique way. The model is better than the example given and accomplishes the project goals more effectively. The model is more useful to the targeted audience through the creativity and innovation of the student.	The model contains a few new improvements that help better accomplish the project goals. The new improvements help make the model useful to the targeted audience.	The model is very similar to the example given by the teacher. The model is still useful but there are no new improvements.	The model was created in a safe manner. The conventional model is not useful to the targeted audience.

Table 5.2
Divergent Boundary Model Rubric

CRITERION	4	3	2	1
Required Elements	The model contains five or more elements of a divergent boundary. The model may contain the following elements: lithosphere, asthenosphere, magma, rift valley, mid-oceanic ridge, oceanic crust, continental crust, and convection currents (elements may vary depending on the type of divergent boundary).	The model contains only four elements of a divergent boundary.	The model contains only three elements of a divergent boundary.	The model contains one or two elements of a divergent boundary.
Element Labeling	All elements are correctly labeled with proper vocabulary and no spelling errors.	Most elements are correctly labeled with proper vocabulary and no spelling errors.	Some elements are correctly labeled with proper vocabulary and few spelling errors.	Very few elements are correctly labeled with proper vocabulary and few spelling errors.
Creativity/ Innovation	The model was constructed and presented in an original and unique way. The model is better than the example given and accomplishes the project goals more effectively. The model is more useful to the targeted audience through the creativity and innovation of the student.	The model contains a few new improvements that help better accomplish the project goals. The new improvements help make the model useful to the targeted audience.	The model is very similar to the example given by the teacher. The model is still useful but there are no new improvements.	The model was created in a safe manner. The conventional model is not useful to the targeted audience.

Table 5.3
Transform Boundary Model Rubric

CRITERION	4	3	2	1
Required Elements	The model contains six or more elements of a transform boundary. The model may contain the following elements: lithosphere, asthenosphere, oceanic crust, continental crust, convection currents, earthquake focus, fault, and epicenter (elements may vary depending on the type of transform boundary).	The model contains only five elements of a transform boundary.	The model contains only four elements of a transform boundary.	The model contains less than four elements of a transform boundary.
Element Labeling	All elements are correctly labeled with proper vocabulary and no spelling errors.	Most elements are correctly labeled with proper vocabulary and no spelling errors.	Some elements are correctly labeled with proper vocabulary and few spelling errors.	Very few elements are correctly labeled with proper vocabulary and few spelling errors.
Creativity/ Innovation	The model was constructed and presented in an original and unique way. The model is a better than the example given and accomplishes the project goals more effectively. The model is more useful to the targeted audience through the creativity and innovation of the student.	The model contains a few new improvements that help better accomplish the project goals. The new improvements help make the model useful to the targeted audience.	The model is very similar to the example given by the teacher. The model is still useful but there are no new improvements.	The model was created in a safe manner. The conventional model is not useful to the targeted audience.

Table 5.4
Volcano Model Rubric

CRITERION	4	3	2	1
Required Elements	The model contains 12–15 elements of a volcano. The model may include elements include the ash cloud, vent, parasitic cone, lava, sill, throat, crater, lava flow, conduit, branch pipe, side vent, magma chamber, magma, flank, and dike.	The model contains 8–11 elements of a volcano.	The model contains 5–7 elements of a volcano.	The model contains 1–4 elements of a volcano.
Element Labeling	All elements are correctly labeled with proper vocabulary and no spelling errors.	Most elements are correctly labeled with proper vocabulary and no spelling errors.	Some elements are correctly labeled with proper vocabulary and few spelling errors.	Very few elements are correctly labeled with proper vocabulary and few spelling errors.
Creativity/ Innovation	The model was constructed and presented in an original and unique way. The model is a better than the example given and accomplishes the project goals more effectively. The model is more useful to the targeted audience through the creativity and innovation of the student.	The model contains a few new improvements that help better accomplish the project goals. The new improvements help make the model useful to the targeted audience.	The model is very similar to the example given by the teacher. The model is still useful but there are no new improvements.	The model was created in a safe manner. The conventional model is not useful to the targeted audience.

The process of creating exhibits involves students continually participating in project-based learning practices. Every student focuses on the significant content, conducts further research if questions arise, and engages in activities that are relevant to the driving questions. When problems arise, students will think critically to find solutions, and communicate and collaborate effectively with others if they are working in a group. Students also develop creativity and innovation skills by continually making new improvements to their work to create the best product possible.

Reflection and Assessment

The unit consists of three separate assessments: two formative assessments and one summative assessment (**Table 5.5**). The first formative assessment transpires after the research portion of the unit. This assessment identifies whether or not students know the significant content of the unit, specifically information about the different boundaries and volcanoes. This assessment can come in the form of exit slips, learning logs, or graphic organizers. The next formative assessment involves students creating digital boundary and volcano models that contain correctly labeled elements.

Table 5.5
Unit Assessments

UNIT SEGMENT	TYPE OF ASSESSMENT	DESCRIPTION
Research	Formative	Exit slips, learning logs, and/or graphic organizers can be administered during the research phase of the unit to identify whether or not they are meeting learning outcomes. These assessments will help monitor the progress of the students' learning before entering the Minecraft phase of the unit.
Creating Exhibits	Formative	As museum curators, students create their own virtual 3D boundaries and volcanoes exhibits to generate more interest from young visitors. The three exhibits must contain all the crucial components of the large-scale systems, as well as identify each component with a correctly labeled sign, and add new improvements and originality to their exhibits.
Video Recording	Summative	Students will pair up and record each other giving a tour of their exhibits. The video captures students identifying and explaining elements of each system, describing what occurs in the systems, and communicating how the elements are interconnected during tectonic activity.

After students are finished with their digital exhibits, they begin their summative assessment, which requires them to video-record themselves explaining their models, identifying system elements, and describing what occurs in each system. Video creation is a great assessment tool because it requires students to use higher-order thinking skills, engage in creativity, develop problem-solving skills, and be actively engaged in their own learning. And of course, the video-making process assesses to see whether or not students mastered the knowledge and skills of a unit.

The assessment begins with the teacher providing an example of what their video should look like. Then students develop an outline of what they would like to capture for their video. The outline is broken up into three sections: introduction, boundary exhibits, and volcano exhibit. The introduction contains a greeting from the student(s) and a description of the project, which includes the driving question, real-world situation, and the culminating product. The next two sections involve students giving a visual tour of their boundaries and volcano, identifying and explaining elements of each system, describing what occurs in these systems, and communicating how the elements are interconnected during tectonic activity. A rubric is given to the students to convey what is expected in their video (**Table 5.6**).

Next, students use their outline to practice what they will say and show in their video. It is recommended that the teacher educate students in elocution, emphasizing the use of a clear, audible voice and correct pronunciation of vocabulary terms. After practicing multiple times, students pair up with a partner and take turns recording each other with their mobile devices at a quiet location in the class or school. As of now, iOS and Android devices do not have screen-recording features that would allow students to record all their onscreen activities for the project.

Table 5.6
Video Rubric

CRITERION	4	3	2	1
Introduction	Includes exceptional greeting and a thorough description of the project that lets the viewer know the driving question, real situation, and culminating product.	Includes a greeting and a thorough description of the project, but does not include one of the following: driving question, real situation, or culminating project.	Includes a greeting and a description of the project, but does not include two of the following: driving question, real situation, or culminating project.	Either the greeting or the description of the project is missing.
Identifying Elements	Every element is identified and explained during the visual tour of their exhibits.	Most elements are identified and explained during the visual tour of their exhibits.	Some elements are identified and explained during the visual tour of their exhibits.	Few of the elements are identified and explained during the visual tour of their exhibits.
What Occurs in Each System	The visual tour provides detailed descriptions of what occurs in each system. The description also includes information on how the elements are interconnected during tectonic activity.	Most systems are described thoroughly with information on what occurs in the systems, and how the elements are interconnected during tectonic activity.	Few systems are described thoroughly with information on what occurs in the systems, and how the elements are interconnected during tectonic activity.	One system is described thoroughly with information on what occurs in the systems, and how the elements are interconnected during tectonic activity.

Sharing the Project

Students share their project using two methods. The first method involves students presenting their videos to their peers. Students are placed into groups of three, where they take turns presenting their exhibits. While a student presents, the other two classmates write down feedback on a slip of paper (**Figure 5.9**). The feedback includes a list of things the students liked about the presenter's exhibits, any new facts they learned, and a suggestion that will improve their exhibits or presentation.

List the things you liked about the presenter's exhibits:

_____

_____

_____

_____

_____

Name any new facts that you learned from the presenter.

_____

_____

_____

_____

_____

Name one suggestion that you recommend to improve the presenter's exhibits or presentation.

_____

_____

_____

_____

_____

Figure 5.9 **Feedback paper.**

The second method uses YouTube, a video-sharing service available for both iOS and Android devices. A slip is sent out to families asking parents for their permission to post their child's video online. The permission slip also specifies that the posted videos would be made *unlisted*, an option that makes videos unavailable in search but still available to be shared via its URL. After installing the YouTube app, students upload their videos using their teacher's account. The teacher types the password to sign in and does not give the student the password (to keep the login secure). Next the teacher places the videos onto a playlist and shares the URL with students and parents. Some parents are fine with having their child's video posted publicly. This option makes the video available in search, making the audience more authentic because of its accessiblity beyond the classroom.

Project Future

Next year I would like to implement an additional method of video sharing. I think it would be great to have the fourth graders teach a group of third graders about the large-scale systems, making their real-world situation come alive. They can act as museum curators, educating young visitors with their informative video or providing a live tour of their exhibits. Providing this authentic audience would increase students' intrinsic motivation in the learning process.

Resources

Listed here are programs and tools that can assist with running and modifying Minecraft Pocket Edition:

- Buck Institute for Education: http://bie.org
- Next Generation Science Standards (NGSS): www.nextgenscience.org/)
- Fourth Grade Next Generation Science Standards: www.nextgenscience.org/sites/ngss/files/4.ES%205.21.13.pdf
- International Society for Technology in Education (ISTE) Standards for Students www.iste.org/docs/pdfs/20-14_ISTE_Standards-S_PDF.pdf

- Minecraft Pocket Edition Wiki: http://minecraft.gamepedia.com/Pocket_Edition
- Minecraft Pocket Edition iOS App: https://itunes.apple.com/us/app/minecraft-pocket-edition/id479516143?mt=8
- Minecraft Pocket Edition 0.9.0 Update: https://mojang.com/2014/06/pocket-edition-0-9-0-snapshot-biggest-update-ever/
- Minecraft Advanced Touch Technology Interface System (MATTIS): http://minecraft.gamepedia.com/Crafting#MATTIS
- Mojang: https://mojang.com/2014/06/pocket-edition-0-9-0-snapshot-biggest-update-ever/
- MinecraftSeeds.co: http://minecraftseeds.co/

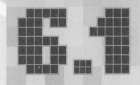

Minecraft and Teaching Humanities

Eric Walker's World of Humanities project was already a big deal in the education world when I first interviewed him, in March 2013. His work has been showcased on countless websites, including, most notably, Time.com. Since I interviewed Eric, the World of Humanities virtual learning environment has evolved and grown more complex as he has mastered the use of Minecraft in his teaching. I can't wait to see what he has up his sleeve for the future.

Eric Walker

I began my career in South Korea, teaching English as a second language (ESL). I continued my work in St. Charles, Illinois, teaching sixth grade social studies and obtaining a master's degree in education. I returned to the adventure of international teaching, working at American schools for expatriate children in the Middle East. I taught at the American International School of Kuwait before moving recently to the American School of Dubai.

I employ a variety of technology in my classroom in my quest to help transform history into an immersive, engaging experience. After researching and testing several educational games and tools, I found Minecraft to be a powerful toolset for creating immersive, and interactive worlds.

Prologue

Sarina stood at the crossroads and stared at the weathered wooden sign-post. In her hands she held a faded and wrinkled map. She tried as best she could to guess her location, dimly recalling last week's lessons on mapping skills.

Far to the left and right stretched tall cliffs made up of cubes of dirt and stone. The sands of the coastal shore wound along with the path to her right. She could hear the gentle lapping of waves mixed with the songs of various birds in the trees high above.

Sarina and her friend had explored this area before, but that was a while ago, and now she was trying to find her way on her own. She hoped to reach the lands of ancient Mesopotamia before nightfall. After all, she had a test tomorrow.

She set off down the path to her right (That's probably east, she thought), following the curves of the cliffs along the shore, until she came to the large, arched opening of a cave. It appeared to lead through the cliffs and out into a wide open bay of clear blue water on the other side. She met a fellow traveler resting on the stones near the cave's exit. She started up a light conversation. He was interested in Mesopotamia too. Sarina remembered yesterday's humanities lesson and found she could actually answer a few of his questions. He even gave her a few coins for her trouble. They were only stone coins, and not very valuable. But she had been saving them, and would soon have enough to trade for a bronze coin. She carefully tucked them into her backpack and continued on.

She passed workers in the fields: the maintainers of the dams and levees that brought just the right amounts of water to the crops, and at the same time forced the small villages to work together and agree on common rules governing the irrigation systems. Sarina asked directions from a field hand and proceeded on her way.

Soon she could see great gold-and-sapphire walls rising from the horizon. After a quick glance at her map, she knew this must be the legendary Mesopotamian city of Babylon. Following the walls to the left, she came across a great gate. Traders and farmers made their way to and from the bustling city. "Ishtar Gate," the sign said. She had seen a picture of this in her textbook.

She stared up at the vast towers and ramparts, blinking in the bright noonday sun. Climbing a set of stairs, she suddenly came face to face with Hammurabi, King of the Babylonians.

Sarina was a bit nervous, she had to admit. Here before her was the king of one of history's first empires. But he seemed more than willing to exchange stories with a simple traveler like herself. The postal service, wasn't it? Isn't that one of the things he invented? Sure enough, Hammurabi puffed out his chest and spoke at length of his great achievements. After a while, he asked her to deliver some letters to the leaders of his empire: governors, members of religious councils, and tax collectors. To her surprise, Sarina found herself curiously interested in the complicated politics required to unite and govern a vast empire.

She collected the letters, made a note in her quest journal for later, and closed her laptop. Her humanities homework complete, she remembered that she had some math homework due as well. She moved her laptop to the side of her desk and pulled out the worksheet.

Project Summary

From the very first day of class, Roger always arrived with a smile, resolved to work hard and do his best. He truly wanted to succeed in humanities (the International Baccalaureate version of social studies), but he found it difficult. More than difficult, actually.

Students like Roger are the true test of a teacher's abilities: students who are willing to work, who will go along with our plans and initiatives, and who truly need the extra help. It was difficult to watch his constant struggles.

I found myself calling on Roger less and less when he would volunteer his answers (which he did often), because I couldn't help but cringe as he confidently delivered answers that were confounding and seemingly random. Some of his less scrupulous classmates would snicker or elbow their partners when Roger participated in class discussions. It even progressed to the point that students would smile or feel sorry for Roger as soon as he raised his hand, even before he spoke. And when he did share, the look on his face as I tried my best to encourage him ("Yes! That's a good idea Roger! And maybe we could also think of...") showed that he knew his own limitations.

He fared much the same in his written work. At the time of the first reporting period, Roger was earning a 3 out of 7 in the International Baccalaureate (IB) assessment scale, which was considered a "failing" grade.

I was of course very concerned for Roger, as none of my instructional interventions seemed to be making much of an impact. It wasn't until he began to explore the World of Humanities that he started to understand the skills and curriculum.

The World of Humanities is a virtual learning environment that I created for my students using the popular video game Minecraft (and the education-focused modification known as MinecraftEdu). I created a virtual world where students could walk around and "explore" their learning, meeting characters from history and embarking on quests that aligned with our standards and curriculum.

As Roger began his explorations in the World of Humanities from his home computer, I immediately noticed improvements. Not only did he display more engagement in class, but it was a better sort of engagement; his discussion participation began to have more meaning and showed a personal connection with the facts, details, and important concepts of my teaching. Other students noticed too.

By the end of the school year, the class would hush whenever Roger raised his hand. They knew that whatever Roger was about to say would essentially be a perfect answer for a future test question. Students rushed to be his partner for collaborative research projects. And Roger was beaming when, just before the end of the year, the progress report showed he had achieved an overall grade of 7 out of 7 on the assessment scale—a rare and noteworthy achievement in the IB system. I had never before seen a student climb from a 3 to a 7 in the course of one year; Roger made the greatest improvement I had ever witnessed as a teacher.

I do not believe that the World of Humanities was solely responsible for Roger's incredible success story. As teachers, we know there to be an incalculable number of variables influencing student performance, and I believe this was true in Roger's case as well. As his teacher, I would attribute as much of his stunning success and growth to his flawless attitude and impressive work ethic as to the World of Humanities. And yet, both Roger and his mother to this day regularly thank me for providing the engagement and opportunity for substantial enrichment that Roger saw in the World of Humanities.

Roger carried his success with him through the following school years, and he improved his understanding and performance in many of his other classes. But humanities became his strongest subject, and the one he loved the most. He had internalized his learning in a way that was not possible with textbooks, videos, or lectures.

Roger and I are far from the first to discover the educational potential of virtual worlds. In an article for the International Journal of Human and Social Sciences, Coffman and Klinger (2007) wrote:

> *Virtual environments have the potential to fully engage students and enhance teaching and learning. They also have the potential to enhance a constructivist learning approach by providing learning opportunities for students that challenge them to learn by experiencing and through applied activities, rather than by direct instruction and passive involvement (p. 30).*

Similarly, neurologist Judy Willis (2011) describes the motivational potential of using educational games and environments to provide incremental feedback and scaffolded instruction:

> *Opportunities for incremental progress feedback at students' achievable challenge levels pay off with increased focus, resilience, and willingness to revise and persevere toward achievement of goals. The development of students' awareness of their potentials to achieve success, through effort and response to feedback, extends far beyond the classroom walls ... application of the video game model to instruction encourages the habits of mind through which ... students can achieve their highest academic, social, and emotional potentials (p. 3).*

That is pretty high praise for video games, which have traditionally been viewed with scorn by many teachers, and have even been considered the bane of students' homework completion.

But the World of Humanities, as designed, is not just a video game. Although it has some structured activities, challenges, and objectives, it is more of a world that students can explore and discover at their leisure.

Whereas other educators have used Minecraft and MinecraftEdu to design very specific lessons and tasks with planned learning objectives in mind, the World of Humanities is a virtual re-creation of ancient history that brings humanities and social studies to life (**Figure 6.1.1**).

Figure 6.1.1
The World of Humanities allows students to explore content and locations from their history lessons, such as this temple from ancient Greece.

When I created the World of Humanities (or WoH for short), I expected it to appeal to and assist only a small segment of my students (particularly those who were already inclined to enjoy video games like Minecraft and World of Warcraft). I was surprised to discover that it was popular with all my students, and that it could contribute to major educational success stories like Roger's.

I have since gone on to share WoH with educators worldwide, and you can explore it with your own students as well. In the following sections, I detail how you can do so. Perhaps you will see similar success stories in your own classroom.

Project Goals

I remember sitting in my high school history class and staring at the walls. I remember thinking to myself, quite deliberately, that there seemed to be some sort of gross injustice being done. No matter what activities the instructor designed, no matter the depth and acuity of the textbook's descriptions and illustrations, no matter the number of fascinating stories and explanations, we were still trapped in a small cinderblock room. It seemed, even to my high school mind, that history was not being communicated sufficiently or with enough depth. Can someone truly understand the horse raids across wide-open Mongolian grass fields, the torch-lit medieval councils, the wooing of a Welsh princess from a tower's balcony? History is far greater than anything that can be delivered within the confines of a painted cinderblock "prison."

Later, as a teacher myself, perhaps my largest objective, my primary and ongoing goal, was to figure out how to deliver the epic realities of history beyond the physical confines of a school. Thinking back to my own wonder as I explored the magical realms of video games as a child, I knew that I had to find a way to merge the potential of virtual worlds with the content and standards of history. Although of course a video game or virtual world is still itself confined to the "prison" of a glowing screen, its power to ignite the imagination while providing interaction and control seemed to far surpass the potential of textbooks and classroom-bound lessons and activities.

When I discovered MinecraftEdu, I thought I might have found the perfect tool to accomplish this. Based on the Minecraft video game, MinecraftEdu was created by Joel Levin, Santeri Koivisto, and Aleksi Postari of Teacher Gaming, LLC. It is designed for educational use, and it provides virtual lesson design to teachers.

I found that some pioneering teachers had already been using MinecraftEdu to design lessons and activities for classes, but I saw in it the potential of world design. I had wanted to create a World of Warcraft-esque persistent environment in which students could log in, explore a variety of units, undertake quests and challenges, find hidden secrets and rewards, enrich some part of their classroom learning, and then log out—only to return later and find that their progress had been saved and was waiting for them. The fact that Minecraft is built with easily manageable cubes—and not the polygons and vertices of other video game worlds—meant that I could better build the world I had roughly envisioned, and that students could leave their own creative mark by modifying existing areas or even building totally new areas on their own. Though I wasn't sure of the technical hurdles I might face, I thought that maybe I could finally immerse students in their history learning by allowing them to explore beyond the walls of the classroom.

Learning Objectives

"Blast you and your World of Humanities!" exclaimed a fellow humanities teacher as he burst into my room one planning period. He was smiling as he said this, however, and so I leaned back, excited to hear what could be the cause of this outburst.

He explained that one of his students had been exploring WoH extensively, and when the teacher had introduced the class's new unit, China, the student had proclaimed, "I already know everything about China—I explored it in World of Humanities!" The teacher graciously yet skeptically accepted this proclamation and continued with the lesson.

But over the next several days he was mildly annoyed, because the student's declaration proved itself to be true. He would begin a sentence of new information only to have the student finish his sentence for him. He said it was as if the student had understood, internalized, and memorized the six textbook chapters that the unit encompassed.

And this indeed was the primary, though somewhat vague, learning objective of the World of Humanities—to include enough engaging content that if a student were to complete everything in the world (going on all the quests, reading all the information signposts, talking with all the characters from history, and so on), it would be as if they had memorized and understood a whole textbook. Everything from basic mapping skills and primary source analysis to the order of ancient Chinese dynasties—I wanted it all to be somewhere in the world, waiting for a student to feel like they had uncovered it on their own.

The main objectives of WoH are the following:

- Increasing engagement and self-efficacy
- Delivering course content and concepts in a method alternative to direct instruction
- Increasing classroom participation via heightened content confidence and prior social engagement within the virtual learning environment
- Improving overall classroom environment and collaboration through prior collaboration within the game world
- Legitimizing of virtual worlds as "real"

The latter three goals touch upon something currently referred to under the umbrella of digital citizenship. Digital citizenship is the educational answer to atrocious YouTube comments sections and the racist, vitriolic ranting of pre-teens over Xbox Live. Anyone who has spent much time in online message forums or engaged in social media debates can attest to the fact that young people are in dire need of guidance and support with their online social behaviors. Digital citizenship is the teaching and modeling of these behaviors.

I was surprised to discover that WoH is almost as effective in teaching digital citizenship as it is in teaching historical content. Students learned, through both positive and negative classroom consequences for their online interactions, that breaking a virtual house that someone had spent hours building is no different from knocking the Lego blocks off a classroom partner's desk. And assisting a new player in an online environment is almost the same as welcoming a new student to the school and offering to sit with them in the cafeteria. As students began to notice real correlations between their behavior in WoH and their performance in the classroom, the congeniality and collegiality of my classroom environment increased noticeably. Encouraging positive digital citizenship became one of my main goals in the continuing management of the virtual learning environment.

But before I could accomplish any of these goals and objectives, I had to create the world in the first place.

Organizing the Project

And there, for several years, ended "free time" as I knew it.

I had quite a daunting task ahead of me: I needed to build the whole historical world that I had begun to envision. As far as I knew from online searches and academic research, nothing similar yet existed. I would have to build it from scratch, and I didn't know whether the world would actually work with our school's computer setup once I had finished it. But I knew there was no other choice: I had to invest the time and creative effort, or else it would remain a "nice idea."

Several factors luckily combined and allowed me to make the immense time commitment needed to properly undertake such a huge endeavor: I did not have a family of my own yet, and the American international school I taught at was in a country with a distinct lack of social nightlife. And so, for several hours each night after teaching, I worked on building the virtual learning environment that I would come to call the Wonderful World of Humanities (**Figure 6.1.2**).

Figure 6.1.2
An overhead
view of the world.

THE WONDERFUL WORLD OF HUMANITIES

The project requires additional time commitment and tools:

- Teacher preparation time: For teachers wishing to use the World of Humanities in their classroom, only a few hours of setup and home testing (exploring the world and preparing some specific introduction activities with students) are required. As for designing, creating, and writing the world and its content, I have spent over 800 hours.

- Project duration: Ongoing. Teachers should expect to spend about three hours a week running and maintaining the world for students.

- Student time spent on project: This varies. A teacher could use the world in just a few in-class lessons, or students could return to the world consistently throughout the course of a school year or more. My own students explored the world in sixth and seventh grades (and many students returned to it in eighth grade and beyond). Some students elected to try it for only a few hours from home, while others played a total of 100 hours or more over the two years.

- Minecraft environment: MinecraftEdu

- World of Humanities home page: http://bit.ly/worldofhumanities

- Other tools: MCEdit, MRemoteNG, FileZilla, DynMap

  These are explained further in the "Resources" section at the end of this chapter.

I began by having Minecraft generate a basic landscape (a "seed") that produced some mountainous islands in the middle of a vast ocean. From the beginning, I aimed to take a more "Disneyland" approach, for playability; students would visit miniaturized replicas of ancient structures and monuments and other themed sections, and could easily travel between them. I did not want to re-create ancient cities on a 1:1 scale, as there would then exist a lot of boring "blank space" that students would be forced to regularly traverse.

I started testing and honing my 3D spatialization skills by building basic structures themed to our units of study in sixth and seventh grades: a treehouse-like starting area that would help teach students the basic controls of Minecraft and would give basic instructions on how to explore and learn within the world, a Greek temple and building spaces for Athenian and Spartan schools, a pagoda-like tower for ancient China, and some pyramids and tomb structures for ancient Egypt.

I soon found out—and any teacher looking to replicate my process for their own custom worlds should take note—that there are several large repositories of pre-built Minecraft structures available online. So I was able to search for "ancient Mesopotamian ziggurat," for example, and find a few options that Minecraft players around the world had already built. It was then a matter of downloading and learning a free program named MCEdit (an external editor for Minecraft worlds that allows for building shortcuts like placing large blocks or spheres within the world; this prevents having to build everything one block at a time) and pasting these pre-built structures into my landscape. Every builder whose creations I asked to use happily agreed when told it would be used for unique and pioneering educational technology purposes. I made note of their names in an authors.txt file that I planned to include with my world files if I ever shared them with other teachers. I also designed some empty areas in which my students could build their own portions of the world.

Even with those shortcuts, I spent countless hours crafting landscapes, forming islands and cliffs, choosing between rock and sand for a coastline, interspersing trees, planning structures, discovering the finer points of interior design when limited to one-meter-by-one-meter cubes, and so on. A teacher-designer should note that there is no substitute for time and practice when creating a 3D world; there is no getting around the fact that designing one will entail a huge unpaid time commitment.

MinecraftEdu allows you to add many custom blocks that are aligned to educational objectives. One of these is the "text block." It looks like an old sheet of paper nailed to a wooden block, and when students click it they are presented with a few short pages of text of the teacher's choosing. I began writing and placing these all over the world, some in areas that were hidden or difficult to reach. I based the information on our curriculum for sixth and seventh grade humanities (common to many U.S. middle schools), which itself is primarily based on the textbook History Alive!: The Ancient World, by the Teachers Curriculum Institute. I included basic facts, fun information, explanations, storylines, and even jokes and riddles for the students to find. I hid code words within some of the harder to reach text blocks, and I planned for the students to be able to collect real classroom rewards (a special reclining chair for a period, their name in the school-wide announcements, a custom-designed printed badge they could pin on a bulletin board, and a corresponding badge for their online profile) by finding these hidden code words and submitting a special "code sheet" with a short summary of the information they had learned while exploring the world. I ended up writing more than 400 pages of text (were you to extract it all into a single-spaced Word document) that encompassed far more than the entirety of our textbook's covered information.

MinecraftEdu is constantly updated, and new features are added regularly (most are at the request of teachers). One feature added later was the ability to have website links in these text blocks. I created some new graphics for a red "link block": a block that students could click and be taken to various games, videos, music, real-life panoramas of historical places, quizzes, and other online interactive features. Over time, I would insert these interactive link blocks in hundreds of locations around the virtual learning environment.

After some initial, successful home testing, I ran the project by my principal and asked for funding. He immediately recognized the potential of the project, and was very supportive. I had already purchased the MinecraftEdu software and one license for $40 out of my own pocket, as I needed to work with the software to begin creating the world.

The costs were not prohibitive (especially for educational software). I would need to purchase one MinecraftEdu license for each concurrent user, meaning one license per student who would be logged in at one time. My school approved 50 licenses, which meant we could have up to 50 students playing at any given moment (but an unlimited number of students could play over time). With the significant MinecraftEdu teacher discount, my school ended up paying about $750. This was a one-time fee; there is no subscription model with MinecraftEdu. For educational technology, I found this to be extremely affordable.

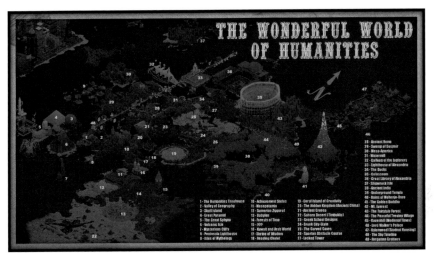

Figure 6.1.3
This map can be printed and distributed to students to help them navigate the virtual learning environment. Students build mapping skills by referring to the map as they play the game. A high-resolution digital copy of this map is available from the main World of Humanities site.

After a few months, I had created enough of the world to begin testing with a group of students (**Figure 6.1.3**). I would later add many features and areas, including the following:

- The Humanities Treehouse. This is a starting area with a tutorial and training section, and teleport stations that allow for instant travel to many important locations throughout the world.

- The Valley of Geography. Students explore common geographical features and read about geographical influence on societal development and agriculture.

- Ancient Egypt. This area contains a pyramid, the Sphinx, an archaeological dig site, and a royal palace, providing a tour of the ancient Egyptian civilization and how modern scientists have rediscovered it.

- Mesopotamia. In this city, students can create an irrigation system and learn about the beginnings of agrarian society, as well as the "seven characteristics of a civilization." Students can carve their own personal achievements into a Mesopotamian achievement stele.

- Ancient Babylon. This area shows the progression from small city-states to early civilizations to vast empires.

- Mali and the Sahara Desert. Here, students follow trade routes to discover the oral traditions of middle Africa.

- Ancient Greece. Students meet the great philosophers who founded Western civilization, and they can work to re-create schools following the educational philosophies of Athens or Sparta.

- Ancient Rome. Here, Julius Caesar introduces students to the complex politics and government systems of a stratified society.

- Ancient China. In this "hidden kingdom," players learn about the advanced technology and rich culture of dynastic China.

- Ancient India. Students make connections between the earliest Indus River civilizations and the spread of religions like Hinduism and Buddhism, and they can attempt to climb a challenging replica of Mt. Everest.

- Medieval Times. This is an introduction to the feudal system and the adventure of knights and castles. Students join a medieval community by building their own houses, or even compete in a non-violent battle arena.

- Meso-America. This island has temples representing the Maya, Inca, and Aztec civilizations. Students observe and possibly join the conflict between the Spanish conquistadors and the indigenous peoples.

- The Great Library of Alexandria. This is a repository of dozens of short stories with connections to language arts.

- The Lighthouse of Alexandria. Students learn about the importance of sea trade in ancient empires, and meet one of the greatest explorers and conquerors of history, Alexander the Great.

- The Fairytale Forest. This dense and mysterious forest is full of the European mythology known commonly as "fairy tales" (with further connections to language arts).

- The Sky Timeline. In this 3D re-creation of history, students "walk through time" and make connections and comparisons between all the historical eras found within WoH.

- Skull Island. This is a scary (but educational) exploration of death and the afterlife myths of various cultures (especially Egypt).

- Isles of Mythology. These floating islands trace a path through the stages of storytelling that originated with Greek myths. They contain a 3D re-creation of the plot diagram, in which students can climb the stages of a story (with direct connections to language arts).

- Volcanic Isle. Students explore connections between humanities and science through the relationships between geography, geology, and conservation.

- Arab and Islamic Worlds. These worlds cover the content our international school was required to teach by the Kuwait Ministry of Education (while making it significantly more interesting, understandable, and applicable to general history).

- Coral Island of Creativity. In this free-building area, students practice their 3D design skills and spatial awareness.

- Carved Caves. This system of underground caves and mines has connections to science through geological features. Students can also carve their own structures into the rock.

- Galleon of the Explorers. Here, students have a chance to meet the great explorers of history, including one of the greatest (but lesser-known) explorers, Ibn Battuta.

- The Mysterious Clocktower and the City of the Future. Students challenge themselves to reach the top of a strange clock tower and find themselves traveling through time to the future, where they make connections between the influences of ancient history and our own modern lives. Students also meet the leaders of two groups in conflict: the Ancient Scholars, who seek to protect the artifacts of the past so that all may learn from them, and the time-traveling Minecrosoft Agents, who wish to sell ancient artifacts to modern private buyers. Students unravel the storyline of their conflict and eventually choose a side to align with, reaping rewards based on their choices.

- Undersea Bio Dome. This area provides further connections to science and illustrates the importance of preservation and conservation for our world and our own history.

WoH is continually expanding, with contributions by students, myself, and others. There are many areas and activities not listed here. **Figures 6.1.4** and **6.1.5** show two pages from an instructions packet I give to my students; they highlight some of the activities that can be completed in the world.

Figure 6.1.4
Students engage
in a wide variety
of interactive
tasks within the
world, above
and beyond
simply rereading
course content.

Figure 6.1.5
Activity illustra-
tions also make
great classroom
decorations.

Getting Started

After the world was (somewhat) complete, it came time for the test: Would it actually work? I recommend that teachers looking to employ WoH with their own students follow the path I did: Begin with a smaller test group of students. I called mine the "beta testers."

But first I needed to place the world on a server that students could connect to from their home computers. A Minecraft server is a copy of the game that runs on a remote machine, either from your school (if your school's network infrastructure allows for this) or from a professional hosting company that will rent out servers for a monthly fee. I had to choose the latter option because of my school's Internet setup.

After trying a few different companies, I found AllGamer.net, a hosting service that allows for full control of the server from home (through a server file structure that is accessed via SSH and FTP). I was able to rent a server with enough power (at least 1.5 GB of RAM and two processor cores) to run the world for about $20 dollars a month. As far as I know, I was the first to create a remotely hosted MinecraftEdu server that allowed students to connect from their home computers. The process is much easier now and is fully detailed on the MinecraftEdu wiki, accessible online.

Once the server was loaded with the WoH files and I could access it from my home computer, it was time to give students access. I sent parents a detailed permission slip describing the project, and I created a set of modified MinecraftEdu files that allowed access only to the WoH server (and not to Minecraft single-player mode or any other online servers). Aleksi Postari, the lead programmer of MinecraftEdu, was instrumental in making this possible.

After distributing the access files to my beta testers, students began to join and explore the world. The feedback I immediately received was extremely positive. Already I could see students making connections to their classroom learning, and becoming highly engaged in the exploration of the content. I created forms that they filled out with feedback, suggestions, and bug reports. I updated the world as they discovered errors or made suggestions for additions.

Perhaps the single largest addition I made to WoH was computer-controlled characters. Karel van Os, a programmer from the Netherlands who goes by the online name Noppes, created a modification for Minecraft that he calls Custom NPCs (non-player characters—a common term in video games). This mod allows for the creation of characters that can travel around the game world, engage in written conversations with players, and send players on teacher-designed quests to retrieve hidden items or speak with other characters. The World of Humanities would not be what it is today without Karel's skillful programming in the creation of this now-legendary Minecraft modification.

When asked about Minecraft's use in modern educational settings, Karel is pleasantly surprised—and proud of his work with Custom NPCs. "I've always seen Custom NPCs more as a creative tool, just like Minecraft itself," he says. "I usually compare it with painting. Minecraft is the canvas and the painting. Custom NPCs is a special kind of brush, to just bring a little more detail to the whole picture, making it more engaging and interactive." He adds, "I had never really thought of my mod as a teaching tool before. It got me really excited, because when I graduated high school I couldn't really choose between teaching and programming. In the end I chose programming, but then with [the mod's use with MinecraftEdu], I saw I was indirectly doing a bit of both. This might actually be the biggest thing I'll ever do in my life, so needless to say I am very excited about it! It's great that new ways are being found to teach children, because I think teaching is done best if the children don't even notice they are being taught. That is probably the ultimate goal."

And so with a mostly complete curriculum presented within the world and, thanks to Karel, a world that had become more interesting and engaging, I was finally ready to open WoH (**Figure 6.1.6**) to the whole school.

Figure 6.1.6
Although students may think they are just playing a video game, they are actually reading a substantial number of non-fiction texts as they navigate the world. This "Great Library of Alexandria" hosts a large collection of short stories that students can collect and trade with other players. Students can also add their own journals and stories to the library.

Completing the Tasks

Would World of Humanities replace traditional education methods, or simply supplement them?

I have a little saying I refer to as "have and half": anything you have to do, you will like half as much. That is, no matter what the activity, if you are forced to do it you will enjoy it less. If a student's homework were to eat a certain amount of ice cream, they would find themselves enjoying ice cream considerably less.

A Supplement, Not a Replacement

It was with this in mind that I originally committed to using World of Humanities in a purely supplemental and enrichment-focused context. It would be completely optional, and aside from my introduction and instructions at the beginning of the school year, it would not take up any class time. Students would optionally connect to it from their home computers, and ideally, many students would enrich their humanities learning through its use. All my more traditional methods of teaching would remain intact, and students would not need to know anything that appeared only in WoH for assessments. I must admit, I partly chose this route for fear that I would face upset parents who had heard that their kid was "just playing video games" in humanities class.

And to some extent, I agreed with that hypothetical parent. If there is a real argument against using video games in education (and I do believe one could be made), it would be that important, foundational, tried-and-true educational approaches were being forgone in favor of a trendy new technological fad. Kids already play tons of video games at home—we have all seen toddlers adeptly manipulating iPad screens at a restaurant table (because the parents just want some peace and quiet)—and there have even been connections made between the seeming abundance of ADHD diagnoses and the increase in young children's screen time.

But as the first year of WoH's use went on, I did not run into any of those hypothetical parents. I did once walk into the school office and have a father, with a rather stern look on his face, abruptly ask me, "Are you the teacher who made that game my daughter is playing all the time?" "Yes, that's me..." I replied, bracing for the worst, and suddenly hoping I could recall the researchers' names I had referenced in my letter to parents earlier in the year. But he smiled widely and went on, "That is probably the best thing I have ever seen done in schools. My daughter loves it. She keeps telling me all the things she has learned as she plays it. I didn't believe her that it was for school at first, but then I saw your letter." He then shook my hand.

As WoH's positive reception increased among students, teachers, administration, and parents, I began to answer my own little "have and half" saying with one a bit less original: You don't know what you like until you've tried it. After all, very few of us would have ever "dabbled" in algebra purely from curiosity. School forces us to try new things, and we discover new talents and learn new skills, and ultimately grow as a person, because of it. Would there be anything so wrong in "forcing" students to try WoH?

Results and Observations

Toward the end of its first year of use, I collected some data from the server's chat logs and assessed the progress of students who had frequently played WoH versus those who had not. Positively, I noted that most of the students who scored the highest on assessments also played the most WoH. But therein was a "chicken and the egg" problem: Was WoH helping students raise their grades, or were the highest-achieving students simply the ones who were the most willing to try new things and dedicate themselves to an after-hours school activity like WoH? Why weren't some of the low-achieving students trying the game? I had hoped it would reach and help them the most.

I also noted that at least two-thirds of the players were boys. I wanted to find the exact reason for it. When I was young, video games were viewed as the preoccupation of, almost solely, young males. But I had thought perceptions surrounding video games and gender stereotypes had changed enough that this was no longer the case (I had heard almost as many girls talking about video games as I had boys, in my previous years of teaching middle school). I wrote part of this off to the fact that my school was in a more conservative environment (the Middle East), but I handed out questionnaires and conducted informal interviews to get to the heart of the reason. What I discovered is that girls view video game playing as more of a social activity, and although WoH is a social game once you are logged in, it is done from a solitary environment (your home computer).

A Balancing Act

So, for the second school year of WoH's use, I decided to blend my approach. It would still mainly be an enrichment tool played from home, and I would not teach any full units of content directly from it, but I would periodically hold "World of Humanities days" at the beginning or end of some units. I had students bring their own laptops into the classroom and guided them through specific content in the game, tied to a unit they were just being introduced to or to review at the end of a unit and before an assessment. This approach was a resounding success.

Students who had never played before, and even some who had shared negative perceptions of it, laughed and called across the room to their friends to come join them on some quest or activity. Girls bunched together around a shared laptop and shouted suggestions to the player. And many more students went on to connect from home and play extensively throughout the year. I had begun to find the balance.

Maintenance and Monitoring

The year continued on, and the required workload tapered off a bit. Aside from major world updates that I created and released every few months, the world and its server required only regular maintenance and monitoring.

Day-to-day server operation is a bit of a tricky business to learn, but it requires minimal effort after a while. Regular tasks involved monitoring the chat, running server commands using an SSH program called MRemoteNG (I have provided descriptions and links to tools in the "Resources" section at the end of this chapter), and reading back through the server logs every so often by accessing the server files through a free FTP program called FileZilla. Eventually I discovered a Minecraft mod called DynMap (dynamic map), which creates a Google Maps–like overview of your world and allows for easy student monitoring from your web browser. The author, Michael Primm, graciously worked with the Minecraft Teachers group to create a MinecraftEdu-compatible version. If I were to guess, I'd estimate that it takes about three hours a week, split into numerous 10- or 15-minute segments, to run and monitor WoH with students.

Ground Rules

I had been worried that I would be dealing with many behavioral issues within the game world. I had seen instances of griefing (purposely annoying other players) in many video games, and I knew that the issue existed in multiplayer Minecraft. But I was shocked at how few behavior issues there were. I had one instance, near the beginning of WoH's school-wide release, of some particularly vile language being used in the chat (not by one of my school's students, but by a cousin of a student, which itself was a big no-no). Many other students immediately rushed in to help. The chat logs were printed out and placed on the assistant principal's desk the next morning, and by that night the child in question was having a very unpleasant chat with his father at the dinner table, chat logs in hand. The story of this got around the school (as I hoped it would), and no serious issues were ever seen again. This process directly illustrated the digital citizenship aspect of the game, with real-world consequences applying to online behaviors (allowing students to see that, yes, real people are affected by our online interactions).

Figure 6.1.7 With thorough exploration, students discover complicated quests and storylines they can engage in. This is the office of the CEO of "Minecrosoft Inc," a shadowy corporation concerned with important artifacts from history.

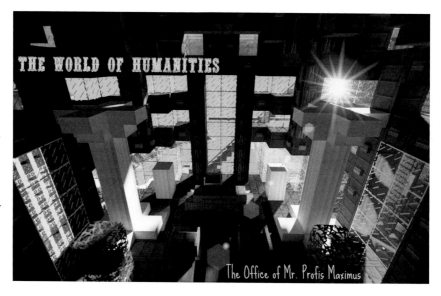

THE WORLD OF HUMANITIES

The Office of Mr. Profis Maximus

The year progressed well. On the "wall of scholars and explorers," badges piled up with the names of students who had found secret codes in their in-game reading. Students who had helped each other build houses or complete quests in the game found each other in the cafeteria and became friends. Girls who had never before played a video game found themselves engaged in the game world, participating in complicated storylines and quest narratives (**Figure 6.1.7**). And some struggling students, like Roger, found their strength and confidence. Not just in humanities, but in academics—and life in general.

Reflection and Assessment

Video games in education are a new approach, so it is difficult to objectively assess their impact. Were you to ask me directly, "has World of Humanities been a success with your students?" the answer would be an unequivocal yes, even though it would be based on mostly anecdotal evidence.

I have had students share answers and discussion contributions that, before they started playing WoH, I would have considered beyond their ability level. I have seen new friendships form, students gain new levels of peer respect as the "experts" of the classroom, and weak students gain confidence in their summative writing. I have had students tell me they thought humanities was going to be boring when they began middle school, but that now it is their favorite subject and they want to study history in college (what have I done?). I have had other teachers share the positive, excited talk of students they have heard in their classrooms, and some have collaborated with me to build areas of the world tailored to their subject areas. I have seen my classroom climate rise to new heights of collaboration with a stronger sense of community and togetherness, and classroom management issues disappear.

But the problem remains that this evidence is anecdotal. I have also seen some struggling students play hours and hours of WoH and make little or no progress with their grades. I have seen a few instances of minor bullying within the game world (though they were quickly dealt with in the "real" world, and most were turned into valuable learning experiences). I have heard students who had never played the game say, "World of Humanities is lame. I like Call of Duty." (Though I guess I should take the comparison to a video game with a multimillion-dollar budget as a compliment.)

David Rempel, a colleague of mine who teaches language arts, worked with me to create a section of WoH themed to one of his units. He created characters, quests, and dialogue that delivered the content and central themes of a novel study unit. He then created two separate formative assessment tasks, one within the game world and one a more traditional reading and writing assignment, and gave his students the opportunity to choose which they would like to complete. After the completion of the assessment activity, he surveyed his students on their experiences and tallied the results. They can be seen in **Table 6.1.1**.

Table 6.1.1
Assessment results

REFUGEE CAMP S.E. SURVEY QUESTIONS	**GAME:** AVERAGE RATING FROM 1 TO 5	**READING:** AVERAGE RATING FROM 1 TO 5
Did you have fun doing this assignment?	5	2
Were you relaxed and happy while working on this assignment?	5	3
Are you now an expert about refugees?	4	4
Do you feel a personal connection to the kinds of people you have learned about?	4	3
Was it easy or challenging to complete the assignment? (Easy 1 2 3 4 5 Challenging)	4	2
Did you see other students finish and do well on this assignment? (No 1 2 3 4 5 Yes)	4	1

This data shows that students were more engaged, more confident, and more empathetic in their learning within the game. Equal amounts of "expertise" were reported between the two sets of students.

But there are two points of particular interest. One is the increased levels of self-reported empathy present in the game players. It would appear that participating in a virtual simulation of learning does indeed lead to greater personal and intrinsic understanding of content than simply reading about or being told the information. Secondly, and most strikingly, the game players reported higher levels of both challenge and engagement. Could video games be that magic but elusive tool that teachers have long sought, wherein the more challenging a task is, the more simultaneously engaging it is? This admittedly small set of data may suggest so.

Sharing the Project

Following the widespread success of World of Humanities in my own school, I decided to share the complete game world, for free, with teachers worldwide. Interested teachers who already own licenses of MinecraftEdu can download World of Humanities for free from **http://bit.ly/worldofhumanities**.

Please follow the installation instructions on that site carefully to get it installed correctly on both teacher and student computers.

Since I began sharing the world with teachers, I have received many reports of success in humanities/social studies/language arts classrooms around the world. The only "payment" I ask of teachers is that they share with me (via the Google Group linked in the site, or through email) their stories and their students' feedback on what works particularly well or what needs improvement. The World of Humanities is a changing entity, and I hope to continually expand and improve it.

Two other items of note for teachers that plan to use the World of Humanities in their classrooms (or with their students via home connections): One, WoH is a malleable world, and the content has been designed with my own students in mind. Feel free to build new areas or modify existing ones to fit your particular needs. I have provided links to editing tools mentioned in this chapter in the "Resources" section.

Secondly, and most importantly, the World of Humanities is not a pre-packaged resource that you can just throw at your students and expect it to work. It takes involvement and a lot of unpaid effort and time on the part of the teacher. Be proactive. Help your students make connections, both content-wise and behaviorally, between the game world and your classroom. Provide thorough guidance for their early explorations; go on "team quests" through areas that match your current units of learning, or create scavenger hunts for items you want them to find.

And lastly, explore the game world extensively yourself before you ask your students to join. The more you explore, complete quests, talk to characters, follow storylines, and so on, the better prepared you will be to guide students through the learning you want them to achieve—and, the more ideas that will come to you of how you might wish to contextualize and modify WoH.

Project Future

World of Humanities is incomplete and always will be. Since the world has gained popularity worldwide, I have received constant feedback from teachers and students. This has led my students and I to create new areas, write new characters and quests, and modify existing challenges and puzzles.

I have created NPC Packets, wherein students write dialogue and describe the appearance of a new character they would like to be placed into the world. Some of these characters are historical persons from our learning, and others are "tour guides" that give advice to new players, based on the students' own experiences and ideas. And through the use of MCEdit, I have had students create schematic files of buildings and structures and then submit them to me in consideration of becoming a permanent feature in the world. Other students, both my own and from around the world, have given invaluable suggestions on how to better hone quests and challenges to become more understandable or complete.

More recent additions include updated graphics through a "shaders" mod, texture replacements based on the Sphax Texture Mod and my own amateur PhotoShop work, and pets and riding creatures through the use of Noppes's other major Minecraft mod, Animal Bikes. I have plans for many more additions and upgrades for the world, most of them led by students and based on student feedback. And of course I will continue to share the updates and additions with teachers around the world via the MinecraftEdu website.

Joel Levin, co-creator of MinecraftEdu, brings up some interesting points when describing his own experiences with WoH. "When I first came across the Wonderful World of Humanities, I couldn't believe what I was seeing," he says. "The world really opened my eyes as to what was possible with MinecraftEdu. Eric had used our version of the game to create something far grander than we, as the creators, ever imagined. It is such an immersive experience with people to meet, puzzles to solve, and secrets to discover. Players can truly get lost in these historical locales. The whole is certainly greater than the sum of the parts."

But he goes on to make an interesting and important analysis of WoH when compared to other instances of Minecraft's use in education. "Different teachers approach using Minecraft in the classroom in a variety of ways. On one end of the spectrum are teachers who are ardent believers that the experience must be student-led, every block should be placed by a kid. Others believe in creating crafted journeys that guide learners along a path, facilitating a set of events designed to impart pre-determined knowledge. I think [WoH] exemplifies the latter approach taken to its ultimate extreme."

Just prior to writing this chapter, the reputation of WoH contributed to my being hired at one of the more prestigious international schools in the Middle East. At this school in Dubai, in addition to teaching middle school social studies, I will be running a Minecraft exploratory class through which students will have a significant role in creating and changing the world. I hope to use this opportunity to further blend the student-led approach that Joel mentioned, to hopefully achieve a better balance: the student-led creation of a deep and immersive world that will help complement and enrich the traditional learning experience.

Resources

Listed here are programs and tools that can assist with running and modifying World of Humanities:

- World of Humanities: http://bit.ly/worldofhumanities (or just search online for "Minecraft world of humanities")

  This is the main WoH page, where teachers can download and install the game world for their students. It includes many links, videos, resources, and tools for the daily operations of WoH within a classroom setting or from students' home computers.

- MinecraftEdu: www.minecraftedu.com

  This is the educational version of Minecraft, created by Teacher Gaming, LLC. I highly recommend teachers use this instead of regular Minecraft, as it includes many useful features and tools for teachers not found in Minecraft itself. They also offer Minecraft licenses at a huge discount for schools. MinecraftEdu is required to play World of Humanities.

- The MinecraftEdu Wiki: http://services.minecraftedu.com/wiki

  This is created by teachers, for teachers. Almost any question you may have about purchasing, installing, and optimally conducting MinecraftEdu lessons can be answered here.

- MCEdit: www.mcedit.net

  This powerful Minecraft world editor is a must for building large sections of a world and for copying and pasting structures (built by your students, or found online) into an existing world.

- Minecraft forums: www.minecraftforum.net

  In addition to being a place you can seek help for Minecraft-related issues, the forums host a ton of modifications, maps, and structures for importing into your server.

- Planet Minecraft: www.planetminecraft.com

  An additional resource for buildings, landscapes, and character graphics. Although these items have been made available for free download, it is in good form to ask the content creators for permission before including their work in your world. And if you share your world with other teachers, don't forget to create and include an authors.txt file containing the creators' names.

- AllGamer: https://allgamer.net

  My chosen server hosting company. They offer competitive prices for renting a remote server on which to run MinecraftEdu and WoH. There are many other hosting companies as well.

- MRemoteNG: www.mremoteng.org

  This free program allows you to log in remotely to your hosted server and manage it through command lines. Though it can be a bit complicated and, depending on your chosen server host, may require some basic knowledge of Linux server operation, only a few basic commands need to be understood to launch and maintain a remote WoH server. For example, the command I use to launch my server is:

  ```
  screen java -Xmx2300m -jar minecraftedu_server.jar nogui
  ```

  This specific command launches the server in a "screen" (meaning you can close MRemoteNG and the server will still be running; use the command screen –r to reconnect later), sets the RAM usage to 2300 MB and launches the Edu server without graphics.

- FileZilla: https://filezilla-project.org

  A free FTP client that allows you to connect to your server to upload your game files or download chat logs and student profiles. This works similarly to a computer's normal file and folder system.

- DynMap: http://bit.ly/dynmapedu

This Minecraft mod (compatible with MinecraftEdu) allows you to view a map of your server from within a regular web browser like Chrome or Firefox. You can easily view student chat and see where they are currently exploring within the world. You can also chat with your students as they play. My students love to view their friends playing while they themselves are away from their computers (since it can be accessed on any Internet device, including smartphones).

References

Coffman, T., & Klinger, M. B. (2007). Utilizing virtual worlds in education: The implications for practice. International Journal of Human and Social Sciences, 2(1), 29-33.

Frey, W., Bergez, J., & Joseph, A. (2004). History Alive!: The Ancient World (Student ed.). Palo Alto, Calif.: Teachers' Curriculum Institute.

Levin, Joel and Santeri Koivisto. MinecraftEdu. Computer software. http://minecraftedu.com. Vers. 1.6.4 build 15. Teacher Gaming, LLC, 23 Apr. 2012. Web. 28 June 2014.

Willis, J. (2011, April 14). A neurologist makes the case for the video game model as a learning tool. Edutopia. Retrieved July 30, 2012, from www.edutopia.org/blog/video-games-learning-student-engagement-judy-willis

Minecraft and Teaching Humanities

I interviewed John Miller in February 2014, but I had been wanting to hear from John and see his Minecraft world for a long time before that. Humanities is a rich subject to use with Minecraft, and John's project is a perfect example of a fully immersive project that engages students and propels them into an ancient civilization. My favorite part was reading the information blocks outside the student-built structures, which students wrote from the perspective of the citizens of that ancient time. I look forward to seeing what John does next with Minecraft in his classes.

John Miller

I began my teaching career 22 years ago along the Central Coast of California. I hold both multiple-subject and single-subject credentials in science and history and have spent my entire career at the middle school level. My interests in technology and gaming led me to persue a master's degree in educational technology from San Diego State University. I am a Google Certified Teacher and enjoy using Google Apps and games with students for learning in my classroom.

Project Summary

As a culminating project for our unit on medieval China, my students and I re-created the Tang dynasty capital city of Chang'an (**Figure 6.2.1**). The Tang dynasty (7th through 10th century) is considered a golden age for Chinese art, literature, and philosophy and is one focus for seventh-grade world history in California.

Figure 6.2.1
The Tang dynasty capital city of Chang'an as built by middle school students in my history course.

The capital city of Chang'an (current city of Xi'an) was considered one of the largest cities in the world at the time, with over one million residents. It was laid out in a formal grid fashion, resembling an irregular rectangle, and was home to farmers, artisans, merchants, governmental workers, and nobility.

The students use a city template that I created—which includes empty streets, market squares, and areas for gardens and a royal palace—to re-create a thriving and geographically significant trading city complete with agricultural and commercial developments and Buddhist temples. Students research social roles during the Tang dynasty and provide biographical sketches for the occupants of each building they create.

Project Goals

Initially, this lesson was developed as a summative assessment for students near the end of our unit on medieval China. However, during the design process it became clear that this project would more than adequately address three broad goals targeting higher-order thinking skills for middle school students.

- Design, plan, and build a historically accurate model of an ancient Chinese city, and populate that city with authentic citizens.
- Use Minecraft to support collaborative learning and decision making.
- Enhance writing skills through visualization and roleplay.

Learning Objectives

The California Content Standards for history and social science, as well as the national Common Core State Standards in English language arts, provide the primary objectives for learners.

Under the California Content Standards, students are asked to describe the development of social order and the influences of Confucianism, Buddhism, and trade in China during the Middle Ages, with emphasis placed on the role of the imperial state.

Writing objectives under Common Core include the development and organization of writing for task, purpose, and audience; the establishment of objective tone; and informational writing through historical narrative.

In addition to these primary objectives, I include personal objectives for individual students, targeting behavior modification, strategies for English language learners, and special education modifications.

Organizing the Project

The project is organized into three stages: information gathering, building in Minecraft, and writing. The entire project took a little over a month to complete and was assigned to 145 students across five history classes. All classes worked collaboratively in the same world.

The project requires some time and tools:

- Teacher preparation time: Approximately five hours in Minecraft, plus an additional six hours for reasearch and lesson development
- Project duration: Four to five weeks
- Student time spent on project: Approximately three weeks learning about China, six days working in Minecraft, and an additonal two to three days for writing
- Minecraft environment: MinecraftEdu
- Other tools: Google Docs, grid paper

Stage I: Information Gathering

During the information gathering stage, I attempted to reach students by mixing modalities for learning. They are expected to read and recite text to themselves and in front of class; listen to, observe, and interact with documentary evidence; write both informally and formally about the subject matter; and perform and interact with one another through classroom roleplay.

Stage I prepared them for building in Minecraft. During this stage I was able to monitor student progress through the use of a shared Google Doc and by reading their written reflections on personal blogs. In addition, I digitally recorded student performances in front of a green screen with other students to check oral language fluency.

Stage II: Building in Minecraft

Most of my students had never played Minecraft before, so I wanted to provide them with a comfortable, low-stress, and collaborative environment in which to build with limited distractions. I used no plug-ins or specialized resource packs.

While researching Chang'an, I found several illustrations online that included a plan for the city. Using MinecraftEdu, I created a flat world and set to work modifying the full-scale template to best fit my objectives. I laid out city streets, created two open-air market areas, and enclosed the city behind a wall with a formal gate (**Figure 6.2.2**). In addition, I set up multiple areas for farmland and grazing outside the city walls.

I zoned each city block by placing a color-coded Minecraft block within each rectangle that identified it as either a residential, commercial, or governmental zone.

Each city block was also numbered so that students could locate it quickly each day. I added a schematic of a large palace to act as anchor, focal point, and inspiration during the student build stage. In addition, I placed three model Chinese-styled buildings outside the city walls so that my students could study architectural details and add them to their own creations.

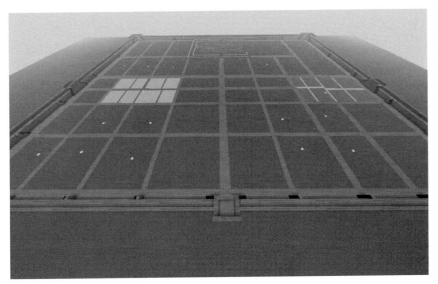

Figure 6.2.2
Students began the build process using this modified city plan based on the original layout of Chang'an.

Stage III: Writing

Formal writing is a challenge for my students. Most are several grade levels below where they should be in both reading and writing, so I created a biographical model and rubric to use with this project.

Using Google Docs, I created and shared the model and rubric with each student, along with a website that generated Chinese names. I placed the rubric at the end of the document for reference. I asked them to use descriptive vocabulary and their knowledge of Tang dynasty culture to write about the occupants of their building in a formal, historically accurate informational style.

Through the rubric, I asked them to provide information about the role of each citizen in Chinese society, job descriptions and occupations where appropriate, information on social status, family history or governmental duties, and how citizens spent their leisure time.

Once I approved their written assignment, students would revisit stage II of the project and place their writing on an information block just outside the door of their building.

Getting Started

After completing stage I of the unit, students had enough background information to begin the building phase of the project. Within each class period, students organized themselves into one of three categories that related to their Minecraft building skills. Most students classified themselves as beginners, about 20 percent described themselves as intermediate builders, and two or three students in each class period identified themselves as advanced players.

With student groups formed, I assigned each a city block and gave them their task.

- Beginners were assigned the construction of multi-family peasant homes at the city's edge and told to fit three or four attached homes within the confines of their assigned block.

- Intermediate users were assigned the construction of single-family homes in the city or peasant farms and pastureland outside the city. A few were assigned to re-create one of two open-air market-places, complete with vendor stalls and chests full of goods to sell (**Figure 6.2.3**).

- Advanced players were tasked with creating the royal garden, a palace for the prince, large homes for noble families, and a Buddhist temple.

Figure 6.2.3 Two open-air marketplaces were created by students and contained items that would have been available to buy during the Tang dynasty.

We began the design process on paper. Students were given graph paper and asked to re-create their assigned block. Next, they sketched out the footprint of each building they were to create, making sure to include enough space between dwellings.

Students then worked in creative mode and were asked to complete building exteriors only. We agreed on a set of building rules and best practices before beginning the building phase, and I reminded each of them of their responsibilities and expectations every day thereafter.

I encouraged students to look at the model buildings provided and to incorporate Chinese building design elements they found by researching online.

The build continued in chronological order by period for six days, with each class getting to see the work completed by the previous four classes.

Completing the Tasks

Students were highly focused on their work, and we experienced very little griefing or off-task behaviors. Students new to Minecraft spent some time getting used to the controls, but by day two, everyone was comfortably involved with their assignment.

The build stage was so popular that I opened my classroom at lunch and had a packed house each day. Students were experimenting with textures, design options, and colors in an effort to replicate medieval Chinese buildings (**Figure 6.2.4**).

Each day of the build began with a quick flyover of the construction site, the sharing of creative building techniques or materials used, or the offering of suggestions.

I saved the world after each class period and made a copy of the map each day in case of vandalism, but I never needed to restore one. At the end of each day I recorded a flyover of the map, which I used to create a time-lapse version of the entire process at the end of the build.

After six days of building, we shifted to writing about the occupants of our city. Students used Google Docs to write and conduct further research. I was able to monitor, edit, and apply feedback in real time to each student.

Figure 6.2.4
Students explored numerous design elements throughout the construction process. Each building included an information block like the one pictured here.

Student builders told me about the crops that were being grown on the farms and what animals could be found in the pastureland (**Figure 6.2.5**). They explained how the principles of Confucianism were incorporated into the world's first civil service exam and what it was like to grow up in a large family within a crowded space.

Figure 6.2.5
Farming has always played a central role in peasant societies, and students are fully able to demonstrate that using Minecraft.

I compared their writing to the model and rubric, and I collaborated with each student during the editing process to produce a grammatically correct document that contained appropriate and historically accurate content.

After I approved their writing, they returned to Minecraft, placed their text on the information block next to the front entrance to the home, park, or place of business they had created, and signed their name.

Reflection and Assessment

Using Minecraft in my classroom has changed my approach to lesson design. It provides me with the opportunity to delve into learning with my students in a way that no other tool has offered.

Students are more open to questions about their work while involved with Minecraft. I can ask them for details about their occupants, to make predictions about the effects of proposed city services or inventions on the populace, or to compare and contrast their city with Rome. They are more involved with their learning than in a traditional lesson.

It can be difficult to get a group of mostly unmotivated students to work toward a common goal, but not with Minecraft. Although the opportunity to "play" Minecraft can be extrinsically motivating for many students, at least initially, it's a wonderful vehicle for self-discovery and intrinsic engagement. My students actively collaborated daily and openly shared their ideas with anyone who would listen.

They were highly motivated and inspired by the work done by previous classes. They challenged themselves to learn more and to be better and more historically accurate builders. They critiqued choices for building materials and debated which blocks to use for greater authenticity.

We began each period with a discussion of topics such as social class and housing, rights and privileges of the upper class, job descriptions, and warfare. We made cultural observations and compared Chang'an with our own society and with those that we had previously covered in class.

The quality of writing was much improved over previous assignments. Students actively came up with details about the occupants of their buildings to fit the model and address the rubric (**Figure 6.2.6**). They wrote enthusiastically about societal roles, feudal parenthood, business opportunities, the privileges of nobility, and the ideals of Confucianism and the promises of Buddhism.

Student writing was formally assessed against the rubric and within each student-generated Google Doc. They used the embedded rubric on the document to assign themselves a score, and I followed up and adjusted as necessary.

Figure 6.2.6
Information block written by a student to describe the civil servant who worked in this building.

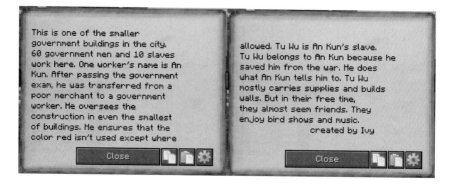

This is one of the smaller government buildings in the city. 60 government men and 10 slaves work here. One worker's name is An Kun. After passing the government exam, he was transferred from a poor merchant to a government worker. He oversees the construction in even the smallest of buildings. He ensures that the color red isn't used except where

allowed. Tu Wu is An Kun's slave. Tu Wu belongs to An Kun because he saved him from the war. He does what An Kun tells him to. Tu Wu mostly carries supplies and builds walls. But in their free time, they almost seem friends. They enjoy bird shows and music.
created by Ivy

Project Future

My students helped me generate several ideas to modify and extend this lesson in future versions. Although I am limited by the number of days I can devote to this unit, I intend to explore many of these options.

I had students write after they built their dwellings because I felt that designing and building a residence within a large city first would help them with descriptive details in their writing. Next time, I would like to reverse that and have them design a building for a family that they have already written about.

With more advanced players, I will give them the option of using the CustomNPC mod, which will allow them to place within their building an interactive character that would answer questions about the occupants or the city.

I will have students create a screencast-produced tour of the city, with segments generated by each group.

As students gain proficiency using Minecraft, I will have them tackle filling in large-scale interiors, which can be a challenge for students new to Minecraft.

I will merge this map with my other Minecraft maps generated for world history. At the completion of this unit, students could pass through the gates, travel north on horseback, and encounter the Great Wall. Beyond that lie Genghis Khan and the Mongols.

As students progress, I'll create a pathway west that would take them along the Silk Road, with building options to support the study of trade and commerce. They would eventually end up in Constantinople and then travel to Florence and learn about Renaissance Italy.

I will explore options for tighter writing integration with language arts colleagues on my campus and with other Minecraft-using educators around the world.

Next year, students will be asked to adopt a persona and, through their blogs, chronicle their adventures traveling through world history.

The famous Terra Cotta Warriors are located nearby, and although they represent an earlier dynasty, it might be fun to incorporate them into this project.

Resources

Listed here are tools that can assist with running and modifying this project:

- Background information on Chang'an: http://goo.gl/BvQx
- Map of Chang'an: http://goo.gl/sK786u
- Digital reconstruction of Tang Chang'an: http://goo.gl/MnlqE1
- Random name generator: http://goo.gl/BoH3
- Schematic models used for student inspiration:
  - http://goo.gl/GczNW2
  - http://goo.gl/CoZ4w3
  - http://goo.gl/gg1MVB
- Original map (empty city): http://goo.gl/C6NCNM
- Completed map (buildings and info blocks): http://goo.gl/pFkfbC

Minecraft and Teaching Science

I interviewed Dan Bloom in January 2014 after I saw an article he'd written on the Edutopia website in December (it took only a month to get together for the interview). Although one of my shortest interviews, it's one of my favorites. Dan had a very concise use for Minecraft, and his experience as a science teacher allowed him to choose a specific challenging experiment that he has his students do every year. His use of Minecraft can serve to tell teachers around the world that not every Minecraft project is vast in scale, and you can create meaningful and engaging activities in small square footage.

Project Summary

Minecraft is becoming more and more popular with educators for its use as a learning tool that enables students to explore, create, and imagine in a completely different way than they could ever before do in a traditional classroom. The beauty of the game is in the way it unleashes the creativity of both students and teachers. But for Minecraft novices like me, it's hard to know exactly where to start unleashing all that creativity. If you're just getting started with Minecraft, it might be helpful

Dan Bloom

I am a high school biology teacher working in New York City. I've been teaching for five years, and I work in a school whose model focuses on game-based education. I have the privilege of collaborating with game designers to add game-like elements to my curricula.

I studied biology at Pennsylvania State University and studied science education at Columbia University, Teachers College. I also completed a year of service with the Americorps program City Year in Philadelphia. I have spent my entire career teaching in urban environments.

to use the game in an activity of your own design. Before jumping into using the game as a creative tool for your students, familiarize yourself with the powerful tools for educators available in MinecraftEdu by building a virtual world for the class to explore. Teachers have to learn a game in and out before using it with their students, and students have to learn the basic controls of a game before using it in a creative exercise. The Minecraft Cell activity solved both of these needs.

For my initial outing with Minecraft, I decided to incorporate the game into my curriculum to meet a specific learning goal: to aid in students' understanding of our DNA extraction lab. Collaborating with a game designer, Claudio Midolo, we devised a pre-lab activity named the Minecraft Cell to provide background for the upcoming lab. In the DNA extraction lab, students practice a step-by-step technique that involves adding certain chemicals to a mixture of cells in order to break the cellular components and isolate the DNA molecules. When I conducted this lab with my classes in the past, I used it primarily for the "wow" factor so that students could see real DNA. But I struggled to find ways to successfully and meaningfully build enduring understanding and connect this lab to the content we were learning in class, or to everyday experiences in my students' lives. As a result, students would walk away from my class with a very shallow understanding of what happened in the experiment.

The solution to my problem was in the delivery of the material leading up to the lab. Claudio and I were able to collaborate to create a pre-lab activity that introduced students to the goals and materials of the lab activity while allowing them to make connections back to content learned in class. In the end, we created a valuable cell model that could mimic real properties, one which students could interact with as if they had been shrunk down in size in order to manipulate the components of a cell.

DNA Extraction Lab

Before describing any more of the Minecraft Cell activity, it would help to understand the DNA extraction lab that we complete in class. For the laboratory activity, we extract the DNA from strawberries. Strawberries are a great material to use for this activity because their cells are octoploid, meaning each cell contains eight copies of the DNA. (By comparison, human cells are diploid, meaning each cell contains two copies of the DNA.)

To begin this process, students seal a strawberry into a Zip-Loc bag, and then they mash the strawberry into a mush. Next, an extraction buffer (a mixture of soap and salt) is added to the strawberry mush, and the students continue to mash up the mixture. The buffer begins to chemically break down the parts of the cell to isolate the DNA. The fatty molecules that make up the cell and the nuclear membranes are dissolved by the action of the soap. The histone proteins that help organize the DNA into chromosomes are broken down by the action of the salt. These chemical reactions are key to breaking down all the cellular parts to isolate the DNA.

Once the strawberry mush has been exposed to the extraction buffer, it is poured through a coffee filter to separate out all the solid components. The liquid component that now contains dissolved DNA molecules is collected in a test tube. The final part of the process is to pour cold ethanol over the top of the liquid. This results in two layers, with the strawberry liquid at the bottom and the ethanol at the top. DNA is soluble in water but not in ethanol, so students witness the appearance of white strings at the barrier between the two liquids. Using a glass stirring rod, they collect the DNA, which appears as white clumps of stringy material. Single strands of DNA are not large enough to be seen with the naked eye, but the clumps that collect actually represent all the molecules of the DNA in the strawberry cells tangled up together, which is why they are viewable.

The Minecraft Cell: Pre-Lab Activity

As mentioned earlier, the lab activity has a great "wow" factor, but without a clear way to connect it to class content, it falls flat in students' minds. I want my students to really understand what they are doing and why they are doing it throughout the procedure. I brought this up with an Institute of Play game designer, and we made plans to use Minecraft to create an experience for students to explore before the lab. Since everything in the lab is happening at a microscopic level that we cannot visualize, we decided to create an experience for the students that would simulate shrinking them down to the size of a molecule and allowing them to tinker with the parts of the cells. In this way, they can interact with the parts of a cell in a way that is not possible in the real world.

When students begin the activity, they learn that their goal is to find their way inside the cell, find the DNA inside the cell, and bring it back outside (**Figure 7.1.1**). They discover several virtual chemical tools: acids, bases, soap, and salt (**Figure 7.1.2**). Equipped with these tools, they try to find their way inside the cell. The chemicals and the cell components accurately interact with each other, so students need to figure out which tools are needed to break through the various parts of the cell. While they are doing this, they are also viewing the parts of the cell and connecting back to class content. When they are finished with the activity, they are able to identify the chemicals needed for the extraction lab, and they can describe how those chemicals help isolate the DNA.

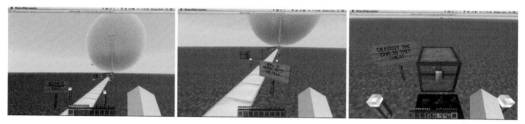

Figure 7.1.1 When students begin the game, they can see the entire cell in the distance (left). As they near the cell, they encounter signs that indicate the goals of the game (middle). At the end, they return to the starting point to deposit the DNA into a treasure chest (right).

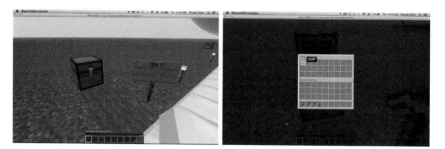

Figure 7.1.2 As you explore the environment when you first enter the world, you encounter five boxes containing virtual chemical tools. Each is properly named and identified on the sign accompanying the box (left) and in the student's inventory (right).

Project Goals

My vision was to create a cell model in Minecraft that students could explore and manipulate. When I did this lab with my students in the past without Minecraft, they walked away with very little understanding as to why they followed those steps and what exactly was happening at a cellular level. This pre-lab activity in Minecraft would allow students to use different "chemical tools" to break down the various parts of the cell and, in the end, identify a list of materials needed to complete the DNA extraction lab. When they do the actual lab activity, they can connect the parts of the procedure with what is happening at a microscopic level.

This lesson occurs after learning content during the "Cells and Organelles" unit, but it serves as a pre-lab activity before conducting the DNA extraction lab.

Learning Objectives

I used to use this lab during my "DNA" unit, for no other reason than students are isolating DNA molecules. But when I really started to analyze the activity, I realized that it connects much better to the "Cells and Organelles" unit. The learning objectives for this lab are as follows:

- Identify the organelles of the cell based on shape
- Identify the chemicals needed to break down the cell parts
- Describe the composition of the cell membrane and nuclear membrane
- Connect soap's function to real-world experience
- Tinker and experiment with materials
- Connect the lab procedure with changes that happen inside the cell

Organizing the Project

In addition to preparing students for the upcoming lab activity, this game also serves as review for our cells unit. I created a student handout to serve as a guide to focus their exploration. In addition to providing instructions for the setup, the handout includes a checklist for exploring the cell and questions for students to answer as they interact with the chemical tools in the cell.

The handout provides students with some direction as they explore, and it also facilitates connections between the game and the class content that they may not notice on their own. We added some organelles to the model that play no part in the experiment, but serve to make the model more realistic. We also created a cell membrane that mimics the lipid bilayer found in real membranes.

The project requires some time and tools:

- Teacher preparation time: Approximately five to seven hours (depending on your comfort level in creating the environment in Minecraft)
- Project duration: One class period
- Student time spent on project: Approximately one hour
- Minecraft environment: MinecraftEdu

Getting Started

Although I am a novice to Minecraft, I was able to work closely with a game designer to create a realistic cell model. Using the MinecraftEdu educator tools, the designer renamed the Minecraft tools with different chemical names. He also figured out how to make some of the materials susceptible to certain chemical tools while being impenetrable to others. Once this mechanic was ironed out, we were very quickly able to create the world of the cell.

One of the earliest decisions we had to make was whether this should be a single-player or multiplayer experience. We decided that single-player would fit our needs so that the cell components could be designed to react or not react to certain tools, and so that each student had the opportunity to tinker and explore on their own, rather than all of them populating the same cell.

When the activity begins, students are spawned at the starting block. Ahead is a massively large cell model, the equivalent of a 20-story building. As they near the cell, they encounter signs that inform them of the goals of the activity, as well as treasure chests full of materials for them to collect. The materials are acids, bases, salt, soap, and the DNA extractor. Two of the materials, acids and bases, are not necessary for this lab but are included as distractions for when the students are tinkering with the materials.

Students are then prompted to climb a massive ladder to a platform that reaches about halfway up the height of the cell. Here, students are faced with finding the right material to break through the cell membrane. They will find that the soap can break the material, and as students pass through the membrane, they are also able to make connections to the composition of the membrane (phospholipid bilayer) that we learned about in class (**Figure 7.1.3**).

Figure 7.1.3 The first connection to the lab involves "breaking apart" the cell membrane. In the lab, this is accomplished with soap. In the Minecraft activity, you approach the membrane (left), are posed with the challenge (middle), and break through the membrane (right). The layers of the membrane are designed to mirror real life.

Once inside the cell, students find themselves in a cathedral-like space. Students are able to identify three major organelles: the nucleus, the mitochondria, and the ribosomes (**Figure 7.1.4**). Although the nucleus is the only one necessary for this activity, the other two are included to test students' ability to identify them based on their shape, another content connection. Next, they make their way to the nucleus and find that soap will also allow them to break through the nuclear membrane.

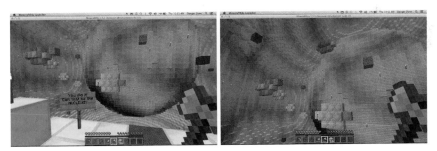

Figure 7.1.4
The environment inside the cell contains three types of organelles described in class: the nucleus (the large central sphere), the mitochondria (green) and the ribosomes (purple).

Inside the nucleus, they are faced with a final challenge of breaking the proteins that cover the DNA molecule. These symbolize the histone proteins that organize the DNA into chromosomes. They tinker with the materials again until they find that salt can break the proteins. In the Minecraft Cell, the actual DNA is represented using spider webs, to simulate the stringy shape of DNA (**Figure 7.1.5**). Students use the DNA extractor (ethanol) to collect the DNA, and then they head back to the starting block to bring the DNA outside the cell.

Figure 7.1.5
Inside the nucleus, you encounter the DNA, which is covered in protective proteins (left and middle). The proteins are supposed to represent the histones of chromosomes. Once you use the salt to break the proteins, you expose the stringy DNA molecule underneath (right).

In the end, we were able to create a single-player immersive world in which students could explore the inside of a cell while using chemical tools to break through and isolate the DNA. They were using their content knowledge to find the DNA, and they were figuring out which chemicals were necessary to dissolve the components of the cell.

Completing the Tasks

The most challenging part of the implementation of this experience is setting up Minecraft on the computers. Because this is a single-player experience rather than a multiplayer server experience, each computer has to have the Minecraft Cell world saved onto it. We set it up as a zip file that students can download from the Internet and save into the MinecraftEdu folder. I provide student instructions for doing this, although not all the students are able to follow those instructions comfortably. Also, when the world has been used once, it must be deleted and reinstalled into the MinecraftEdu folder so that it starts from the beginning again. I spend 10 to 15 minutes of the class period helping students get the world properly loaded on their computers before they are actually able to start. We have been exploring ways to simplify the process in the future.

Overall, students are highly engaged during the activity. While this is my first time using Minecraft in the classroom, it is also the first time many of my students have ever used it, so this activity is also a great way for them to practice using the controls and getting a feel for the game. The students have the opportunity to use different chemicals on the cell parts as if they were shrunk down to the size of molecules and actually tinkering themselves.

Reflection and Assessment

The questions on the handout provide a way for me to assess my students. I am able to see if they can make connections back to course content (review), and I also get a clear picture of whether they are able to meet the learning goals and identify the chemicals needed for the lab. By the end of the activity, they have a clear understanding of the changes the cell goes through during the DNA extraction lab, so that when we actually complete the lab in class, the students feel comfortable talking about it and can successfully explain why we use each chemical.

The activity is a resounding success. Student engagement is at an all-time high. Students who feel weak in science class are able to approach the subject in a way that feels comfortable for them. Some students who were new to Minecraft struggled in the beginning, but quickly picked it up through a brief tutorial from a Minecraft regular. All students are able to approach the content from a unique perspective, as if they are actually manipulating the parts of an actual cell.

Project Future

My students ask me often when we will use Minecraft again in class. This first project was a stepping stone for me, as I had never used Minecraft before and did not understand its potential in class. The Minecraft Cell is a very effective way of creating a designed experience for the students. It has a very specific goal, while also providing support and experience for the students so they can be ready to use Minecraft as a creative tool. I plan to continue using this experience every year as preparation for the DNA extraction lab. But I have also been developing other ways of using Minecraft that allow students to create unique products that connect back to classroom content.

I have already rolled out two projects that involve the use of Minecraft as a creative tool. In one, students build models of organisms and represent body systems inside those models. In the other, students create sustainable ecosystems that include a certain number of organisms, and they are come up with population estimates based on the limiting factors. In both activities, my students came up with very creative and unexpected ways of representing their projects.

Minecraft is a powerful educational tool. It can be a great way for teachers to create a unique experience for their students. It can also be a great way for students to create products that reflect their mastery of a subject, which I am still learning how to do effectively. No matter how it is incorporated, there are countless uses for Minecraft in the classroom.

Resources

Listed here are programs and tools that can assist with the Minecraft Cell activity:

- Student handout with instructions how to install the Minecraft Cell program: www.dropbox.com/s/6u8jcifntgd5po1/5.%20MineCraft%20Cell%20Activity.docx

- The Minecraft Cell activity file: http://q2lschool.org/cell/biogenCell2.zip

Minecraft and Teaching Science

I was catapulted into a huge animal cell in Stephen Elford's Minecraft world back in March 2013. It was my first time exploring an object at such a vast scale in Minecraft. I thought about the movie Innerspace and all those educational cartoons that shrunk the characters down so you could see what was going on at a microscopic level. There are a vast amount of learning opportunities with such miniature adventures in Minecraft.

Project Summary

There is an odd explosion—all the research completed and compiled by the scientists is lost. Although you are only beginning your study of science, you are now tasked with repeating the experiments that the scientists performed and making a report to the government of our Minecraft land about the outlandish statement that Minecraft's gravity is unrealistic.

Welcome to Gravity Lab, a place to explore the gravity in Minecraft, measure its effects, and determine how similar virtual gravity is to real-world gravity.

The idea behind this project came from an experiment that I performed with students in MinecraftEdu. In it, I tested their

Stephen "EduElfie" Elford

I'm a science and mathematics teacher at a secondary college in Northern Victoria, Australia. I've been a teacher for 10 years but a gamer for my entire life. My focus area in science is biology, and I enjoy seeing the "lightbulb" moments that come from teaching science. I very much enjoy working with students and helping them learn new skills that I've never swayed in my choice of career.

I've been using MinecraftEdu in my classes for nearly three years, and I'm a prominent member of the online community of Minecraft teachers. I'm a moderator of the Minecraft Teachers Google Group and an almost permanent member in the MinecraftEdu online support room.

reaction times in the virtual world by dropping them from great heights. This started me thinking about how I could use a similar experiment to measure the speed of gravity in Minecraft, whether the gravity in the game acts on all items and blocks in the same way, and how this compares to real-world gravity.

Instead of just performing the experiments or getting students to perform them, I thought that this might be a good opportunity to create a back story and have students roleplay the job of a scientist and perform the experiments.

Project Goals

Seventh grade students (12–13 years old) study forces. Normally this topic involves experimenting with real-life forces, including gravity, and then presenting the findings to the class in some way. In previous years, students had not overly enjoyed the forces topic, as it can be dry and boring. Usually their final presentations to the class were of a passable standard, but far from fantastic.

The major goal of using Minecraft to perform this project was to increase student engagement by completing a roleplay. By doing this in a game that the students had enjoyed in previous projects, I also was hoping to see a higher level of enjoyment throughout the activity and felt that this would improve student understanding and outcomes.

One other goal was to introduce and discuss the scientific method (a very dry subject). By making the students "live" it, I was hopeful that they would gain a more in-depth understanding of how important it is to consider good scientific practice when completing experiments, most importantly using repetition to remove or minimize errors in gathered results.

Learning Objectives

Through group discussions and experimentation within the game, students were expected to learn about the following:

- Scientific method
- Forces

- Gravity in Minecraft and how it is similar to and different from Earth's gravity

As a byproduct, students also learned about:

- Collaboration
- Calculating averages
- Collating results
- Interpreting results
- Making concluding statements about experiments
- Listening to, reading, and following instructions

Organizing the Project

Having performed experiments "on" students in a virtual world before, the next logical step was to give students the opportunity to perform experiments in the virtual world. I felt that allowing students to hone their scientific method and experimentation skills in a virtual world might be beneficial, and more engaging for them.

At the beginning of this process I needed to explore how gravity behaves in Minecraft and perform some tests to determine whether students would get the information they needed to be able to compare the virtual gravity in Minecraft to the real gravity on Earth. This meant performing the experiments and calculations in Minecraft on my own prior to discussing this possible project with students.

As a class we began learning about forces, discussing the various types of forces in our natural world, how they affect us, and how we can utilize these forces for our own purposes. Later, instead of getting the students to design their own experiment on forces, we began to focus on the force of gravity and how we could explore that through experimentation.

It was at this point that I introduced the idea of exploring the virtual gravity in Minecraft, revisited the scientific method, and explained to students that we would be doing something that I had never done before in any of my classes: a roleplay, where students would actually take the role of scientist in the virtual world. I would be the "head scientist" that students would submit their results and interpretations to. The students reacted with positive excitement to the idea.

The project requires some preparation in terms of tools and time:

- Teacher preparation time (from scratch): 10 hours
- Teacher preparation time (using my map): 1 hour
- Project duration: 2 weeks (but recommend longer)
- Student classroom time spent on project: 90 minutes (but recommend 180 minutes)
- Minecraft environment: MinecraftEdu (for added information blocks, build allow areas, and border blocks to prevent students causing server lag)
- Other tools: Calculator, stopwatch

Getting Started

I created a randomly generated Minecraft map and then chose six different test locations, each with its own unique landscape and objects clearly visible. I then built the test stations at each location. The reason I chose six different locations was because I wanted students to measure the difference between dropping the following: blocks (sand and gravel), items (feather and iron), and entities (villagers and sheep).

As I was building the dropping locations, I decided that there should be six different heights for students to test, three at each location (**Figure 7.2.1**). I wanted students to interpret—and perhaps use some calculations to determine—whether the speeds were the same or different for each pair of blocks, items, and entities.

The sand blocks were dropped from heights of 20, 40, and 60 blocks, while the gravel was dropped from 30, 50, and 70 blocks. The reason I chose to have three different height stations at each location was not only so that students would have to calculate their results, but also so that we could have the added discussion point of terminal velocity by talking about the following questions: Did things fall the same speed the entire way down? At approximately what height did they stop accelerating? Is terminal velocity present or absent in Minecraft, and how do we know?

At each test location I also set up a teleport location so students could easily transfer from one test location to another once they had completed the timing tests. These teleportation buildings displayed the story of that particular location, what the students were dropping, and some lighthearted jokes.

Figure 7.2.1
A test location—
note the three
vertical pillars of
differing heights.

The last step for building the test locations was to restrict students to only the test location. If students wandered off into the distance, the server would slow down, making the measuring of time extremely difficult because the server and clients might not sync properly (which might cause things to happen almost instantly, not flow smoothly). Border blocks in MinecraftEdu make it possible to restrict play to designated areas.

As a central meeting point, considering the back story, I also built a secret underground bunker where students would begin their learning journey. When students entered the world, they appeared in the underground bunker and were instructed to take a seat in the briefing room. An older group of students and I recorded a corny introductory video that I showed the students to set the scene and allow students to begin their roleplay (www.youtube.com/watch?v=PEgu2YA5Xs4).

Completing the Tasks

Students began the first in-game lesson in the underground bunker. As they were logging in and joining the world, I explained that the lesson we were about to do was something that none of us had done in a formal classroom before, and that it was all being recorded to be published and shared on YouTube. I also advised students that it would be very easy for me to slip out of the head scientist character and back into "Teacher Elfie."

So with the stage set, I put on my acting hat and became the head scientist. I told the young scientists that we needed to get started as soon as possible—the government needed our research data quickly (**Figure 7.2.2**).

Figure 7.2.2
Seated at the briefing, ready to begin the roleplay.

Once the young scientists were settled in the briefing room, I explained the task that students were expected to complete, showed them the briefing video, and spent a few minutes explaining the urgency and setting up the roleplay.

I requested that students work in pairs, as that is how the now deceased scientists were seen to operate. I explained the limited knowledge we had about the experiments they were performing, handed out their experimental journals, and let them go to their first test site. I reminded them that if there were already too many people at that site, to go to one of the other sites instead of waiting and wasting valuable time.

The students were given a real-life stopwatch and instructed to bring their calculator to class. Each pair was to switch between the role of dropper and timer, to give them a turn at each role.

The actual task involved students gathering the item or block that was being tested at that site after reading the information available on information blocks. These blocks also provided more back story (**Figure 7.2.3**).

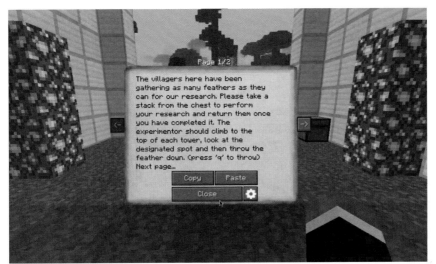

Figure 7.2.3
An information
block detailing
the back story of
this location, as
well as providing
a reminder as to
the instructions
for completing
the experiments.

Once students had gathered the resources and their real-world stop-watches, one member of the team would scale the ladder to the top of the dropping platform while the other waited at the bottom of the pillar, facing but not directly under where the item or block would be dropped.

Working together, students timed how long it took for the item to drop from the top to the bottom. They recorded the result in their in-game journal (**Figure 7.2.4**).

Figure 7.2.4
Students
recorded their
results in an in-
game journal.

As good experimental procedure, they were asked to repeat each drop three times for each of the three heights at the test location. Students were originally asked to complete this for each of the six test locations, but the experiments took much longer than I anticipated, and most students completed only two or three test locations with the requested repetitions.

Once students had begun their experiments, they were mostly self sufficient. One test site did not work. Despite my knowledge about what should happen, some blocks would not drop. I spent some time within the lesson attempting to fix the offending station, but due to a glitch in the software, that station had to be removed from the pool of stations students could use.

With an odd number of students in my class, one student was left without a student partner. I paired with that student, which meant I was able to give suggestions and relevant information. I gained insight into how the activity worked as a student, and discovered what I could do to improve their experience while working in the virtual world.

Reflection and Assessment

Time became our biggest enemy; what I estimated to take 90 in-game minutes and 90 out-of-game minutes quickly expanded to 135 in-game minutes, and many students still had not finshed testing all the locations.

The class time spent outside Minecraft was unfortunately limited to 90 minutes. This time was used for general discussion of the scientific method, a discussion based on our results, and what we as a group discovered and how this compared to real-life gravity. Because of these time restraints, students did not get the opportunity to produce a final report.

Without a final report, students were informally assessed on the in-game journals they submitted at the end of the last session. I gave them this feedback verbally. Students were also anecdotally assessed on their participation in the class discussions and their concluding statements.

Since I used Minecraft in my class and the other science teacher did not, I made the formal assessment in my class a written test, which ensured an equal assessment across the classes and ensured that both classes could keep working through the curriculum without taking too much time away from "normal" classes. I should note that this project was very early on in my integration of Minecraft into my classes—and the staff and administration at my school are now more on board with my use of MinecraftEdu in the classroom.

Sharing the Project

This project was unfortunately only shared locally within my school, with the other seventh grade science teacher. As a team, we ran the same Minecraft activity with the other class. This class also had limited time to complete the activity, so their final output was also limited.

The activity was shared on my blog, in-game class video was shared on YouTube, and the world will be available for download from the MinecraftEdu world sharing site (http://services.minecraftedu.com/worlds/) once it is updated to work with the newer versions of Minecraft.

Other members of the MinecraftEdu community have taken this idea and altered it to suit their students and circumstances—mostly for students to explore gravity in Minecraft and then discuss the differences between it and Earth.

Project Future

I have not repeated this project yet, but I will do so when I teach forces to junior science students again. I plan to alter a few things, such as the time allocated to the project. Two weeks was not long enough, considering that I had students for only 135 minutes a week. I'll be allocating three hours to the in-game sessions and probably the same to the discussion and writeup of the report. With this additional time, the project will be more complete and students will be able to present their final report and findings.

To assist in time saving, I'll look at ways to reduce the travel time for students to reach the top of the dropping platform—by using more teleport blocks, for example, or perhaps the elevators that are available in some Minecraft modification packages.

Overall, the project was a good activity to include in the forces unit, and with these minor adjustments it will be an excellent final assessment piece that students can share with the class, their parents, and the wider community.

Resources

Listed here are tools that can assist with running and modifying this project:

- MinecraftEdu: www.minecraftedu.com
- Blog: http://minecrafteduelfie.blogspot.com.au
- YouTube: www.youtube.com/eduelfie
- World download site: http://services.minecraftedu.com/worlds

Minecraft and Teaching Math

I had my first experience with the concept of teaching math in Minecraft while interviewing Stephen Elford in March 2013. One of the first exercises I took part in while talking with Stephen was to work out the probability of various animals falling down a chute! I could never imagine being so engaged with probability back in my school days, but there I was having a blast waiting for the next animal to fall from above. That was just one of many exercises Stephen has created in Minecraft to teach math.

Project Summary

We have been stuck on this planet since our ancestors' spaceship crash landed here five generations ago. Luckily they found the underground tunnels and escaped the toxic planet surface before they all perished. We have been living in these alien tunnels since then, but we have not wasted our time. We have finally pieced together enough of the history of this ancient race and what happened to this planet that we now have renewed hope and possibly a chance to leave this forsaken planet.

Stephen 'EduElfie' Elford

I'm a "tech head," and I enjoy integrating technologies into my classes to help students learn and to make the experience as fun and interesting as possible. From games to 3D printing, I will try anything at least once in my classroom.

I've been using Minecraft-Edu in my classes for nearly three years and am a prominent member of the online community of Minecraft teachers. I'm a moderator of the Minecraft Teachers Google Group, where teachers can find information and support. I am also a member in the Minecraft-Edu online support room as well as working with the development team from TeacherGaming, suggesting new features to make MinecraftEdu easier for teachers to integrate into their classes.

Here is what we know so far: The race of beings that inhabited this planet abandoned it after a war broke out and destroyed the balance in the atmosphere. There was huge upheaval on the surface, and only those living organisms that could escape and survive underground had any chance of long-term survival. We've also found out that not all members of this ancient race left at the same time; they left in stages, and those that left first carved a path along the planet's surface to the spaceship launch bay for others to follow.

We've translated some texts that say this path is safe to travel for those who know its secrets, but they do not give any specific details on how to safely traverse the planet's surface. It is also written that in order to launch a ship you must gain the approval of something called the Central Database along the way, but there are no details as to how to do so.

You've been chosen to travel this ancient path in the hopes that there are still some ships that we can use to leave this planet and find a new home among the stars. Good luck!

The idea for this Measurement Map project sort of flowed from a project in MinecraftEdu that I had completed the year prior: Mathlandia, a land where math was the way to move forward. A mysterious place of strange beings who always seemed to need help with math, but that also offered great rewards for those who took the time to assist. Mathlandia was intended to be a year-long project in which students in eighth-grade math (13–14 years old) would be able to play within the world during lunch times, but would also join this world and embark on quests during select class times throughout the year.

Unfortunately, as with so many things within a school, time constraints limited my ability to get this project fully functioning. We did, however, perform three quests within the world and also some others external to Mathlandia. Two projects within the Mathlandia world were the basis of this project: the "Perimeter and Area" quest and the "Volume and Surface Area" quest.

Both of these were successful in their own right, but I wanted to improve them and bring them together into one amazing experience. Also, with the successful level of engagement I had in previous roleplay-type lessons in Minecraft, I felt that immersing students in a lesson in which the learning was part of a story would be a good way for students to review the topic of measurement.

Project Goals

Normally in eighth-grade math, reviewing at the end of a topic will include writing a summary book containing important formulae and examples of questions while completing chapter review questions, or practice tests. Students find this quite boring and complete it superficially, just to satisfy the requirements of the lesson, not to better their understanding prior to the test.

So the main goal of using this Measurement Map is to increase student engagement in the review process. To achieve this, the Measurement Map was designed to get students to perform various perimeter, area, and volume calculations, as well as convert between linear, area, and volume metric units.

Learning Objectives

Students are expected to cover the following concepts, which they have already covered during class time in a traditional setting with teacher instruction and consolidation through completing questions from a book.

- Perimeter
- Area of squares, rectangles, circles, triangles, parallelograms, trapeziums, and kites
- Volume of cuboids, triangular prisms, cylinders, and irregular prisms
- Conversion between linear units, area units, and volume units

Organizing the Project

The classroom teachers use the standard techniques for teaching the topics, using examples and questions from the students' text books, as well as some physical models to aid in students' understanding. The Measurement Map comes into the picture as an end-of-topic review.

MinecraftEdu was chosen as the base for this project because it allowed students to have continuity in play, allowed easy input of information into the added information blocks, and allowed easy designation of particular areas for students to build in.

I decided early in the planning for this project that in the "blocky" world of Minecraft I would need some visual assistance for some of the shapes I wanted students to work with; for example, triangles and circles. To get the images that were required for question prompts into the game, I added the Paintings++ modification to the Minecraft install on all student computers.

I then needed to create images for the questions in a simple paint program and place them into the appropriate location in the mod textures file (**Figures 8.1.1** and **8.1.2**). To aid me in placing these paintings within Minecraft, I also added a mod called Forge Paintings GUI, which allowed me to select the paintings to display instead of the random selection that normally occurs for paintings in Minecraft.

Figure 8.1.1
The textures file for Paintings++. You can see the math-themed images.

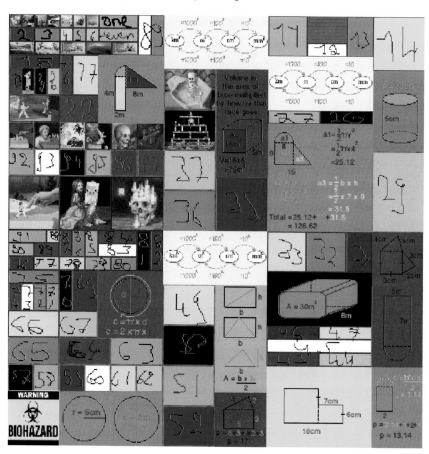

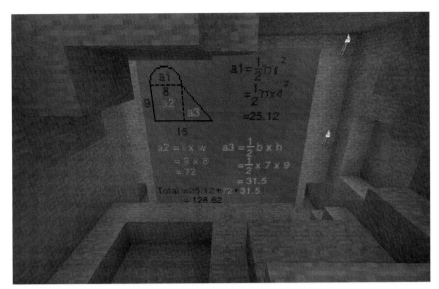

Figure 8.1.2
An example of
how the images
were shown
within the game.

There were two more mods added to the install: Custom NPCs (to allow students to interact with virtual characters that would help them on their journey) and Bibliocraft (to give students access to an in-game measuring tape, and to give me the ability to store students' in-game journals in a text file on the server).

With all the required mods installed and confirmed working, it was time to work on the map. Minecraft's normal terrain generation was not going to be appropriate for the storyline I had in mind. So the map needed to be custom made in an external tool called WorldPainter. I generated a high mountainous terrain mostly out of stone, with some snow on the mountain peaks. This terrain was then flooded so that disconnected islands were left above the waterline (**Figure 8.1.3**).

A printed copy of this top-down view was used to design a path over, through, and between the islands, with the goal of keeping the different "sections" of learning on different islands. Once I determined a basic path that had the rough space I required for each learning section on separate islands, I began work on the background for the storyline and did some very intense testing to ensure it would achieve the goals I required in terms of student review. The essential background items and the reason for implementing them were:

- A scoreboard system that would count up if a student strayed too far from the path. This meant that I could track a student who was wandering and not completing the tasks.

- Permanent night was enabled on a night with no moon so that the lighting was more customizable. I also felt that it made the whole world a lot more post-apocalyptic.

- A second scoreboard system that used the "straying" data to warn students who were straying from the path; if these warnings were not heeded, the student was sent back to the start of the world. This was done so that students would lose progress in the map if they chose to spend too much time away from the tasks they were supposed to be doing.

Figure 8.1.3
The overhead view of the base world created in WorldPainter.

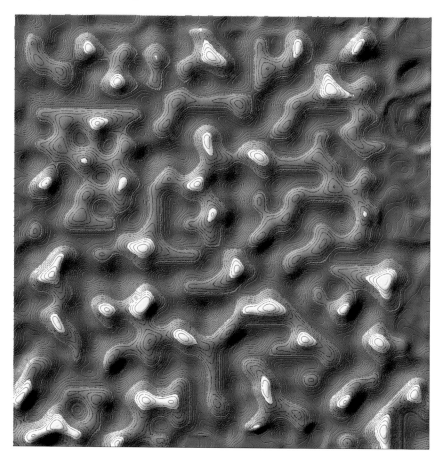

These scoreboard systems used the command blocks found in Minecraft. These blocks can be used to manipulate the experience for students at an individual level without teacher interaction at the time. In the past I had used these blocks to give students items, teleport them around the worlds to where the learning acitivies were, and remove items from students. I had also used these to track student data, record student responses to multiple choice questions, and reward them based on their correct response or require them to complete a similar, second question to improve their understanding if they did not achieve a correct response.

This time however I wanted to take the use of these blocks a step further. I wanted to use these to allow individual student experiences to be different based on their progress through the map. I also wanted to design activities that relied on students estimating the answer to a calculation, submitting that to a scoreboard, and then receiving the number of blocks they estimated in return.

These command blocks in the Measurement Map were also used to track student progress through the map, guide students using informational text, create personal effects on their virtual avatar, and intiate actions based on the stored information about that student.

As an example, I had a checkpoint at the end of each learning section that would "tag" a student as having completed that section. After this, if they happened to be sent to the start of the map because they had strayed too far from the activities for too long, they could teleport directly back to that checkpoint because a particular door would open for them since they had been tagged. This door gave them access to a teleporter to take them back to their most recent checkpoint, this ensured that students did not have to traverse the entire trail again.

All these background items allowed a backstory to be set (which is detailed in the "Project Summary" section). The surface of the planet needed to look extremely toxic; this toxic-looking terrain was achieved by using WorldEdit. I selected large chunks, or sometimes the entire island, and used the `//naturalize` command to make the top layer grass. Then without clearing the selection, I used the `//replace` command to swap the grass for varying ratios of toxic looking blocks from Minecraft (**Figure 8.1.4**).

Figure 8.1.4
The toxic-looking surface created with WorldEdit commands from within the game.

The supposed safe path across the surface was dotted with what were called "safe posts." These ancient posts were made to detoxify the area around them as well as heal those nearby. So that students would be mostly self sufficient, I started students at the beginning of a tutorial area, where they would be able to speak to NPCs (non-player characters) to learn about the various aspects of the game (**Figure 8.1.5**).

Figure 8.1.5
The view students have when they join the world. This is the introductory section of the map, which sets up the backstory.

Students were asked to submit their journal to the Central Database at the end of each island, which corresponded to one section of learning. Due to the nature of the book copying block of Bibliocraft, students could very easily submit their journals but would also have it returned to them afterward. That way, I had a copy of their work in a text file on the server, and students still had the original journal with their character in the game.

With the map, backstory, and background mechanics all tested, I was ready for students to enter the world. Students were given one 45-minute session to become familiar with the controls of Minecraft.

The project requires some prepartaion in terms of tools and time. Here are some tools and timeframes that are needed:

- Teacher preparation time (from scratch): 30 hours
- Teacher preparation time (using my map): 3 hours
- Project duration: 2 weeks
- Student classroom time spent on project: 180 minutes
- Minecraft environment: MinecraftEdu (for added information blocks and build allow areas)
- Other tools: Calculator, WorldPainter, WorldEdit, Bibliocraft

Getting Started

When we began this project in class, the students had not been in a formal Minecraft lesson before. In fact, many had not played except for that 45-minute overview of the controls that I gave them. I needed to give students an introduction to the expectations of learning within Minecraft, and how their behavior in this task would affect their ability to complete more of these tasks.

With the boring but essential stuff out of the way, I put on my best storyteller's hat and explained the storyline to the students. I explained that I was trying something new and that all the information they needed for completing their tasks was either already in the game or already in their workbook—so I was going to respond to any question with "Have you read all the instructions?" and then follow with "Have you checked your workbook?" If the answer to either question was no, I would tell the student to revisit the relevant information. Many students are all too eager to be given the answer rather than trying to work it out for themselves. So instead of telling them the answer, I forced them to find it on their own.

After all the explanation, students were free to begin the activities. It was expected that during the remaining time in the first lesson, students would finish the tutorial island and then begin the Perimeter one so that in the next lesson they could log in to the world and go straight to the tasks (**Figure 8.1.6**).

Figure 8.1.6
Students being taught how to use their measuring devices by an NPC (Spencer).

Completing the Tasks

The actual tasks the students are to complete in game vary from finding and copying down important rules for performing calculations (**Figure 8.1.7**) to applying these rules to questions (**Figure 8.1.8**).

Figure 8.1.7
Students are prompted by Control to copy down the rule for calculating the perimeter (circumference) of a circle.

Figure 8.1.8
A choice in which students have to apply the previously acquired rules for the area of quadrilaterals.

Other tasks require students to use their measuring tape to calculate the lengths of sides, and then use these lengths in their calculations (**Figure 8.1.9**). Others require students to perform a calculation, submit their answer to the Central Database immediately to receive that number of blocks (**Figure 8.1.10**), and then use the blocks to build the required shape and test their calculation (**Figure 8.1.11**).

Figure 8.1.9
Students measure the length of the sides of these squares and then calculate the perimeter.

Figure 8.1.10
An "estimation station" where students submit an answer and receive that number of blocks in return.

Figure 8.1.11
Students are asked to build a bridge over a chasm using the blocks they receive from the Central Database.

I designed the tasks so that students could be mostly self sufficient, and rely on me only for dire problems. This meant that students would get input from Control (the humans who have sent them on this quest) or from Central Database, and I could wander the room helping students with questions or advising them of the direction they were supposed to head.

But I found that students, as they had not been in a lesson like this before, could not contain their enthusiasm for exploration, much to the detriment of their understanding of how to complete the tasks. Many students ran straight past all the computer characters in their eagerness to explore. I spent far too much time directing students on "how to do the tasks" instead of "how to do the math."

I had allocated approximately 45 minutes (or one lesson) per section, allowing time to revisit the expectations for the second session, and again for the third and fourth session. Students did improve over the lessons, but the total of about three hours in game resulted in only two students completing the entire path, and most others completing about half of it.

The idea behind getting students to submit their in-game work was so that I could print them out and students could use them as their summary book when they were tested on the topics. Since only two students completed the entire path, I, unfortunately, had to write a summary sheet to give the students for the test.

But not all was lost. The tasks were self directed and required limited teacher input, so I was able to wander the room, supporting students at their point of need, because it was clearly visible when students were having trouble completing the tasks. Also, some of the questions inspired excellent discussions on using predictions to determine whether or not a calculation was likely to be correct.

Reflection and Assessment

As a separate task, students were asked to complete a survey before the project and again after the project to determine their perceived level of knowledge and also their feelings about using Minecraft as a learning tool. I used this data to inform my teaching practice and my planning for more Minecraft lessons.

At the end, students had a much more realistic understanding of their own level of knowledge. Many had overestimated or underestimated their own understanding, but by going through the activities in Minecraft they gained a much clearer indication of their true level of understanding.

Students did complete a standard pen and paper test at the conclusion of the project, and I provided students with verbal feedback on their in-game journals. Although it was not part of the original goal, students made considerable progress on the skills needed to learn in this kind of activity, an activity to which they had not been exposed. Although this task was not an outright success in terms of mathematical learning, it was a positive learning experience for all involved.

Sharing the Project

I wrote about this project on my blog (http://minecrafteduelfie.blogspot.com.au) and discussed it with members of the Minecraft Teachers Google Group. The world will be available for download from the MinecraftEdu World Library site after adjustments have been made to the background mechanics.

Project Future

This project will be adjusted based on student feedback and teacher concerns before being run again. One key adjustment will be that I'll add more building/interaction questions. I would like to incorporate the standard pen/paper test into this map to allow students to test their knowledge. Only through successful completion of this test will students be able to launch their spaceship to a new world.

I would also like to record a video of the backstory from within Minecraft. I think this would set the scene much better for students in a wider range of classes, as well as making it easier for teachers to use this map in their classes. It would be as if they were viewing the recent history of their race in a briefing before heading out on the journey.

Resources

Listed here are tools that can assist with running and modifying this project:

- WorldPainter: www.worldpainter.net
- Paintings++: www.minecraftforum.net/forums/mapping-and-modding/minecraft-mods/1287285-1-7-2-subarakis-paintings-no-more-bugs
- Bibliocraft: www.bibliocraftmod.com
- CustomNPCs: www.minecraftforum.net/forums/mapping-and-modding/minecraft-mods/1278956-custom-npcs
- MinecraftEdu: http://minecraftedu.com
- YouTube: http://youtube.com/eduelfie
- Blog: http://minecrafteduelfie.blogspot.com.au

Minecraft and Teaching Math

I wandered into Shane Asselstine's Minecraft world for the first time in December 2013. It is a vast and exciting map—so vast that he and I saw only a few areas during our interview. The time and effort Shane has put into this world to instill engagement and excitement in his students is inspiring. I loved spawning at Shane's school campus to start off our exploration and can only imagine that his students feel the same way.

Project Summary

The focus for classroom instruction is technology and mathematics, although I will stray into other subjects if they integrate with the lesson. Each week I see about 240 third- through sixth-grade students for two 45-minute periods. I work closely with the homeroom teachers and discuss the topics being studied to make sure that we are all on the same page. The students come to my computer lab, and then I reteach, review, and extend the learning, with a focus on constructed response for mathematics.

Traditionally, math lessons were paper-and-pencil-based worksheets or Powerpoint presentations. Over the past few years engagement in the lessons has diminished, so I began to search for an alternative. Minecraft had been mentioned a few times

Shane "MisterA" Asselstine

After careers in architecture and information technology, I returned to school to get my master's degree in education. I've been very fortunate to work at Momilani Elementary in Hawaii for the past decade, teaching fourth grade for several years before moving into a curriculum and technology role. I've been playing and learning from games for most of my life, and it seems my previous experience has lent itself well to the integration of MinecraftEdu into my classsroom lessons. I am an active member of the MinecraftEdu community and share many of my maps on the MinecraftEdu World Library.

by students in passing and again by my aunt in California. She was a teacher for over 35 years and has always been a mentor for me. She mentioned that Minecraft might be something that I would enjoy using as a teaching tool, and she wasn't wrong.

Researching Minecraft and MinecraftEdu resulted in hours of play time, involvement in a very active community, and a wonderful professional learning community group that includes many of the people writing this book. MinecraftEdu provided an opportunity for me to meet kids where they are learning while covering the mandatory math standards and making education fun again. The option to learn in an online collaborative environment was appealing and exciting to say the least. As far as I knew, no one in the district was offering anything like this, and my administration was very supportive. Ultimately, I made the decision to incorporate MinecraftEdu into the teaching.

I introduced it at the end of the 2012–2013 school year as an after school option, just to see how it would be received by students. Very quickly word got out that the computer lab had Minecraft, and kids came in strong numbers from third to sixth grade, boys and girls. I had seen in my research that another teacher had re-created the school campus, and this was what I wanted to do first. The goal was laid out for the after school students, and they worked on the school campus for the next month. This experience solidified MinecraftEdu as a geniuine learning tool.

I spent the entire summer going through the game, playing, taking notes, learning, and building. I worked out ways to use gameplay mechanics and what makes Minecraft so special to cover most of the newly adopted U.S. Common Core State Standards (CCSS) standards from third through sixth grades within MinecraftEdu.

That school year, I fully integrated MinecraftEdu into my classes as a learning tool. Students interact and work collaboratively in an online world to provide them a method of learning that could not otherwise be accomplished. Just as I did before MinecraftEdu, I continue to work with some of the best teachers, and we decide on the math topics for the week. The difference is that now, instead of spending time creating worksheets or presentations, the work begins on creating a map with several activities to support and extend the learning.

I use the school campus, now known as the Momilani MCEdu Project, as the base for all of my lessons. We created an area called the Neighborhood on the edge of the school campus, and students were given a 10x10 piece of land to call their own. They could use the land to build themselves a home, keep valuables, and display personal items. Although this seems like a small thing, the effect that this has is incredible. They learn life skills such as responsibility, socialization, community, and they feel more invested in the virtual world.

Each week, when the classes come to the computer lab, the students log in to MinecraftEdu and we start on the school campus. They come to the bank and are paid in-game currency for any work they have completed before we move on to the next lesson. They use the currency they receive to purchase in-game materials to build Minecraft homes, completing the economic cycle. Each classroom in the virtual school has a portal device installed and is used for that grade level to teleport to the lesson worlds. So while students head toward the classroom, I place the dimension book into the portal device to activate it. Once the teleportation device is activated, students walk through the portal to teleport to the lesson of the day. To date, I have created over 30 lesson worlds for students. The topics range from multiplication and division to graphing and statistics.

In one of the lessons (the one we'll focus on in this chapter), students teleport to a "sky-block" map called Sky Tree Farms (**Figure 8.2.1**). This fifth-grade map focuses on metric conversions of linear units through three tasks related to tree farming. The tasks are delivered using MinecraftEdu information blocks. Students right-click the block to read the contents. Each task challenges students to use the skills and procedures related to converting units.

Figure 8.2.1
A view of the Sky Tree Farms map from above. Be careful, that first step is a doozy!

Project Goals

I am always looking for ways to improve my teaching and engage students in the learning, and MinecraftEdu was a tool that I felt could do both those things.

Providing students with another option for learning content can sometimes make a big difference. Sometimes the lessons are the primary delivery method, and sometimes it is for reteaching and reviewing, but many times the goal is to apply concepts and demonstrate understanding.

With the Sky Tree Farms map, the goal was to have students apply the concept of metric linear unit conversions through three tasks, the biggest of which was a set of building directions with a variety of units. Students work collaboratively in groups of three to four to complete the tasks on the map, practicing communication and cooperation throughout the lesson (**Figure 8.2.2**).

Figure 8.2.2
Stating the standard and setting the tone for the map through storytelling or a brief description of the map contents.

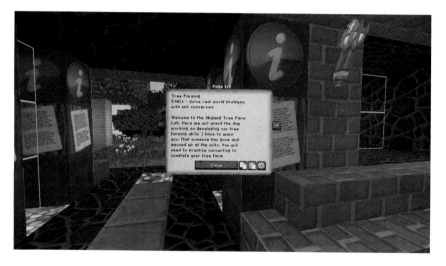

Learning Objectives

This lesson focused on a specific standard: CCSS 5.MD.1.

"Convert among different-sized standard measurement units within a given measurement system (for example, convert 5 cm to 0.05 m) and use these conversions in solving multi-step real-world problems."

Within this lesson map, students are expected to read and analyze information blocks, signs, and results from their actions (**Figure 8.2.3**). This is an important skill for many subjects—not just in math—and an integral part of the way this map works.

Figure 8.2.3 The key to the map is in reading the information provided.

Each of the three tasks requires that students use multiplication, division, and place value to convert metric linear units of measurement.

Ultimately students were expected to use these conversions in solving multi-step real-world problems—in this case, solving the problems from the three tasks related to the tree farming lesson.

Although we don't have formal technology standards in Hawaii, at our school we choose to use the ISTE standards as a guide. This type of project definitely provides opportunity for the students to demonstrate the following standards:

- Digital citizenship
- Communication and collaboration
- Technology operations and concepts

Organizing the Project

The map layout in any lesson forms itself, but there are factors I take into consideration when creating a map. For instance, I prefer to include a variety of ways to learn within the game, such as game mechanics, research, and data collection, among others. Then I decide how students will demonstrate the learning. Most of the time there are word problems in the information blocks, a build/gathering exercise, and of course the learning journals. When delivering a task, I think of three ways to do this with students: individually, in small groups, or as a class.

The project required some time and tools:

- Teacher preparation time: Approximately 12 hours
- Project duration: The project is year long but this lesson takes about 90 minutes to complete.
- Student time spent on project: Approximately 1.5 hours
- Minecraft environment: MinecraftEdu
- Other tools: MCEdit and World Painter

World Settings

World settings for each map within the Momilani MCEdu Project can vary from Survival mode to Creative mode, but for the most part we play in MinecraftEdu mode. This mode is a hybrid of Creative and Survival. You still have all the functionality of Survival mode but without the death and hunger worries. I have created maps with persistent day or persistent night, but for the Sky Tree Farm map, night and day cycle was important to the growth of the trees—it all depends on what you are trying to accomplish in the map and how those settings will help achieve that. The map does not require any modifications, or mods, but the use of a minimap mod such as Zan's Minimap is helpful for navigation.

Spawn Point

Throughout the Momilani MCEdu Project, students are teleported to a variety of worlds with a wide range of environments. Each of the maps uses the spawn point as a familiar starting point for the map. The spawn point is a common area students will spawn into after teleporting from the school campus classroom portals. The spawn point acts as a central point for the formalities of the lesson: getting a book and quill that we refer to as a learning journal, submitting the journal, as well as teleporting in and out of the map. They get their learning journal by clicking one of three buttons under the signs labeled "journals." This causes a command block to execute a give command to the nearest player. It starts out as a blank in-game book that students set up with a title page, and continue to write in as they go through the lessons. Once the learning journal is set, they go to the information block to prepare for the lesson (**Figure 8.2.4**).

Figure 8.2.4
Pick up your learning journal to the left, and submit it into the chests on the right when you have completed the tasks.

This setup did not come instantly; there were at least four or five iterations. The first was just for teleporting—as I was just getting a handle on how this whole thing would work it seemed the most necessary. After a while I added the ability to get a journal, which we used as in-game learning evidence. Finally, after a few tears and lost journals, I added the submission system that allowed students to turn in learning journals before leaving the map.

The spawn point also serves as the final destination of the students and a place for them to turn in the learning journals. There are three chests on one side for students to submit their learning journals to the teacher. A system has been set up using hoppers to transport the learning journals to a single hidden chest, where only the teacher has access. This prevents students from tampering with each other's learning journals.

Before students leave this area, there is an information block that sets up the story and the tasks for the lesson.

Map Layout

The map is custom-created; I used a tool called World Painter combined with in-game World Edit tools. Within World Painter, I created a mountain and then created a schematic. Once that was done, I created a fresh new void world, and used World Edit tools to import the schematic and invert it. This created the platforms of land. It is laid out in a simple cross pattern. It contains the main floating island with the spawn point, surrounded by four other floating islands (**Figure 8.2.5**). The area surrounding the islands is a void, so anyone who falls into it will be gone; they will of course respawn at the spawn point. Depending on your class, you may find it valuable to enable the `keepInventory true` command so that if students fall off they still have the learning journal.

Figure 8.2.5
An island in the
middle of the air?

Information blocks are located all around the map to guide students in their learning. To ensure that they are easy to find, each information block is identified with an "information sign" above it.

Getting Started

After setting up the fifth-grade classroom for teleporting to the proper world (lesson) for the students, I instruct them to come to the classroom.

Before students teleport away on a new adventure, we always discuss expectations, guidelines, and groupings. We cover what to do when they arrive on the other side, review how effective online collaborators work together, reinforce being good citizens, and (if we are working in groups) cover the groups they are in for the lesson. Then, they go through the portal and into the new world.

Students arrive on the other side of the portal and begin to prepare the learning journals. Each journal should have a title page, so students fill out the first page with number, name, and date. This allows teachers to track the journals in case students forget to sign them before turning them in to the chest.

As the rest of the students read the first information block, one brave soul reads it aloud to the class. This information block sets the tone of the map through storytelling or by setting the students on an initial task. Many times students will run past it or take extra time to set up the learning journals and not get the foundation for the map, so having someone read it out loud helps to ensure they have this information. Then students are on their own. At this point, facilitating and providing minor directions are my goals. A handful of students will always have questions. Many times, just refocusing on reading the directions will solve the problems.

It takes several lessons for students to become used to the process. The first time they teleport, there is usually chaos and questions and noise. Once they arrive in new worlds, they take off or start trying to dig. They all try to cram in front of one of the buttons that give out learning journals and complain they are not getting one. Through practice and time, they learn to line up and be better digital citizens. This whole process and setup for my spawn point is definitely a preference and has evolved from my first few maps. It has gone through many iterations and may still go through more as we see a need to change it. Some teachers just choose to spawn into a world and use the command line or the teacher menu of MinecraftEdu to accomplish the same results. I feel that having the students be a bigger part of taking care of themselves has numerous advantages and provides for intangible learning, such as citizenship, cooperation, and self-management.

Completing the Tasks

The structure of the tasks within my MinecraftEdu maps are adapted from a combination of curriculum-based word problems and in-game, hands-on activities. Utilizing the game mechanics was top priority— I didn't want to educationalize something that the students loved so much; I wanted to capture what engages them and use it to teach. Each task provides students with a different take on problem solving.

The first task requires students to learn about the trees they will be using. Familiarizing the students with the types of trees provides background knowledge for those students who do not play Minecraft, while refreshing details for those that do. The information about the trees is delivered in an information block just outside the bridges to the floating islands. Students take the information about the average heights of three tree types (provided in different units), and using conversion they order the trees from smallest to largest. For example, the average oak tree grows to be 10 meters tall, the average birch tree grows to be 700 centimeters tall, and the average jungle tree grows to be 0.026 kilometers tall.

The second task, and definitely the most interactive, is to create a tree farm. A tree farm is an advanced Minecraft tactic that uses the game mechanics to grow trees in a confined area. By understanding the mechanics, a player can maximize the amount of wood that can be gathered efficiently with the land provided. Students plant many trees in a small area, while still providing the required space and lighting for growing the trees. The advantage of this is that students do not need to work as hard to gather plenty of wood resouces. The students work collaboratively on this, emphasizing communication and organization and naturally forming roles. The directions for creating the tree farm are written on signs in the build areas on the floating islands (**Figure 8.2.6**). All the necessary supplies are provided in this area. The directions are given in mixed-up units, and students are required to convert them into something they can use for construction. Once the tree farm structures are built, the students wait for the trees to grow.

The final task relies on group collaboration and successful completion of the tree farm. Students chop down all the trees in the tree farm and calculate how much wood the tree farms produced. Then they use that number to solve the final word problem, in which the students are asked how long, in kilometers, would the wood be if were laid in a line.

Figure 8.2.6
Follow the directions, or you never know what might happen!

Although this lesson was scheduled to be only one 45-minute block, it actually took two 45-minute blocks to complete. The extra time was due to waiting for trees to grow, correcting errors from conversions, following directions, and documenting in the learning journals. In the end, the additional time was well worth it because the results showed that many students were able to complete the activities and demonstrate understanding of the topic through the builds, discussions, and learning journals.

Reflection and Assessment

Students were assessed in multiple ways throughout this lesson. Utilizing the information blocks and creating a self-directed map style empowered the students and allowed me to assess in ways not possible with traditional methods.

Several oral discussions happened during this lesson, including about the life cycles of trees, sustainability, and the importance of reading directions. All of which led to a greater understanding of how this lesson fits into the world around us.

Students liked the immediate feedback they got while the teacher flew around and observed them. Through observation, both in-game and from walking around the room, you could see the formation of roles, the collaboration efforts, and the product. One group had jungle trees, and they decided to plant them before building the roof for the tree farm—the result was a huge jungle tree that took them forever to cut down. Had the students followed directions, the roof would have prevented the trees from growing too tall and unruly (**Figure 8.2.7**). Other groups had trouble with the conversions, which was apparent just by flying by and seeing the shape of the base they had constructed. A few words of instruction to these groups and they were easily back on track (**Figure 8.2.8**).

Figure 8.2.7
You may have missed a step somewhere!

Figure 8.2.8
Four proud students, one complete tree farm.

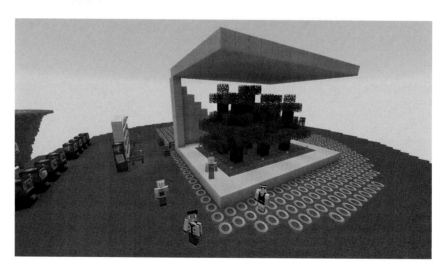

Last but definitely not least, they were assessed using the learning journals (**Figure 8.2.9**). Each student turned in a learning journal, which was corrected by the teacher and assigned a value based on completeness and accuracy for the next week's payment.

Another piece of unofficial assessment for the teacher is the reflection blogs that students write about the experience of learning conversions in MinecraftEdu. These are not formally assigned to students; instead, they are the writings they choose to do on their own. Many students use a reflection format (that they learned earlier in the year) to share what they like and dislike, and even what they feel they have learned. This is extremely helpful when making improvements to the map.

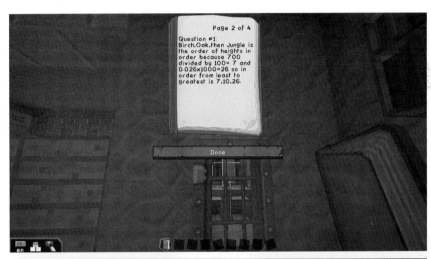

Figure 8.2.9
Journals are a primary source of assessment after the lesson is completed.

Sharing the Project

Using MinecraftEdu in the classroom allowed for an interesting way of sharing work. Our virtual school library (**Figure 8.2.10**) is filled with these student-created learning journals. The learning journals contain calculations, written explanations, and other forms of learning evidence. Each student has a virtual shelf to store completed learning journals. These journals have been used to show teachers and parents growth in student work throughout the year. They have also been used as exemplars to demonstrate the quality of work that is expected.

Figure 8.2.10 Providing each student with a virtual shelf in the school library to display learning journals allows for an interesting sharing opportunity.

Project Future

The project has definitely been a success. Students are engaged, the lessons are being learned, and there is fun again in the classroom.

However, some aspects of the lesson need to be addressed:

- The downtime between the tree farms being completed and waiting for the trees to grow was not anticipated. Do I introduce bonemealing to increase the growth rate, or not? What issues might it cause?

- Should students spend some time researching the best layout for a tree farm themselves, before entering Minecraft? Although this would increase the time required for the lesson, it may be a wonderful way to integrate some English language arts standards based on applying informational text.

- Future iterations of this map will include non-player characters (NPCs) that will provide the information about the trees in the first task. Something like, "Talk to the three lumberjacks about the types of trees, then answer this word problem."

- Presently for the building task, students are given unlimited amounts of building materials (**Figure 8.2.11**). It might be interesting to introduce scarcity and limited supply. The lack of materials would produce a built-in temperature check of how they are doing. If they run out of something, maybe they have to reevaluate what they have done so far.

Figure 8.2.11
Sometimes less is more—maybe I should provide a finite number of resources to the students.

Resources

Listed here are the map, mods, and other relevant links that can assist with running and modifying this project:

- Map Download—http://services.minecraftedu.com/worlds/node/50
- Zan's Minimap Mod—www.mediafire.com/download/ fctjzgq71e8lr9d/ZansMinimap1.6.4.zip
- Map FlyThrough—http://youtu.be/ZVvUbOle-oM
- CCSS Standards—http://standardstoolkit.k12.hi.us/common-core/ mathematics/
- ISTE Standards—www.iste.org/docs/pdfs/20-14_ISTE_Standards-S_ PDF.pdf

Minecraft and Language Learning

James York appeared on my Minechat series in February 2013 and then again in November 2013. His Minecraft world has evolved so much over time that I felt that we needed an update, and I can only guess there will be future visits to his Kotoba Miners Minecraft world. I always cite James's use of Minecraft as a jaw-dropping example of Minecraft in education. I guess many people have struggled at some point to learn a second (or third or fourth) language, but how on earth can Minecraft assist with this? Read on.

James York
I am an assistant professor of English at Tokyo Denki University, Japan. As part of my job, I teach an elective seminar class once a week on a research subject that I am interested in. This Minecraft project started during a seminar class in which I was using it to teach Japanese students to speak English. The project quickly expanded, and now the Kotoba Miners project includes a course for people to learn Japanese.

I have a master's degree from the University of Leicester and am working on an EdD. My research is concerned with the development of a suitable teaching methodology to promote oral language proficiency in virtual worlds.

Project Summary

言葉 (Kotoba):

noun

1) a language; speech; (a) dialect

2) a word; a phrase.

miner 1 | ˈm ɪn |

noun

1) a person who works in a mine. A coal miner.

Based on these definitions, the idea behind Kotoba Miners (KM) is the use of Minecraft as a domain for the acquisition, or mining, of words—or more importantly, language, specifically Japanese and English.

My history with language learning in virtual worlds and with the use of games started in 2005, when a friend asked me to start playing World of Warcraft (WoW). I had just moved to Japan and was just beginning my adventure with the Japanese language. I knew that WoW would drain any free time that I had, but I didn't want to give up learning Japanese, so I made a compromise. We decided to join a guild of Japanese players. This experience was invaluable on my journey to fluency and started my interest in the subject of online communities for language learning.

I am now teaching English at a Japanese university and conducting research on the use of games in language education. The head of my department told me that I could do a seminar class once a week on anything I wanted, so I decided to make my research into a class: learning English with video games.

But why Minecraft in particular?

I experimented with a number of virtual worlds and games as part of my research. I rejected massively multiplayer online games (MMOs) for lack of control over content and their often extremely specialized discourse (for example, Prot Warrior LFG SFK pst). I also rejected a lot of social worlds (such as Second Life) for their painful aesthetics, controls, and perceived distance between "users" and "content creators." That is to say, they appeared to be either one or the other rather than both.

Minecraft is simple. From controls to aesthetics and even gameplay. This means that you spend less time learning how to navigate the game and more time learning and focusing on language. Additionally, it gives teachers and learners 100 percent control over content—content that is easy to create and use. All in all, it is a very appealing canvas for the creation of language learning activities and of locations for language practice.

The KM project differs from other projects you will find in this book because it uses a Bukkit server (https://bukkit.org/) that is open to the public at all times. In other words, the KM server is not on a LAN, is not white-listed, and is not restricted in any other way. It would be difficult to conceive of the project in any other way, and the reason for this will become clear in the following pages. And although part of this project does take place in an educational institution, the main student body is made up of individuals outside of school or education, and most are adults with full-time jobs.

Project Goals

The main goal started out as: Provide a safe, motivating, and immersive environment for my Japanese students to learn English.

However, this goal drastically transformed over the first six months of the project to what it is now: Provide a safe, motivating, and immersive environment for my English-speaking students to learn Japanese.

This does not mean that the original goal has completely disappeared—I still teach English to Japanese students on the server—but I now focus more of my efforts on teaching Japanese. Why? We need to go back to the start of the project to understand exactly what happened and take a moment to consider and respect the phenomenon of emergence in online communities.

The server was initially set up with a few basic lesson ideas and activities to help my students learn English. It had no additional plug-ins and no security until a player from Finland offered to help me out. I gave him admin access soon after, and he is still with the project to this day. Next was to find English speakers to participate. I asked on the popular news website Reddit whether people would be willing to come onto our server once a week to help my Japanese students learn English. As part of this, I also mentioned that as my students' level of English was fairly low, the experience would also be a good opportunity for them to practice Japanese. The results were very positive. Once a week, my students logged in and completed activities with English-speakers that came from Reddit. Once the course finished, my students stopped playing on the server, but the native English speakers continued. I was suddenly faced with a server of English speakers who were interested in learning Japanese. It was this experience that started my interest in teaching Japanese and led to the creation of Kotoba Miners.

Learning Objectives

There is a unified test for assessing Japanese ability, much like the Test of English for International Communication (TOEIC). This test is called the Japanese Language Proficiency Test (JLPT), which has five distinct levels: N5 through N1, where N5 is the easiest test and N1 the most difficult. The objective of KM is to enable students to pass the N5. Although there is no speaking component on the JLPT tests, the Japanese course I designed has a strong focus on speaking. The reason for this is that learning in a virtual world lends itself to social learning, where interactions with peers provide a fantastic opportunity to develop communicative competence.

Organizing the Project

The main tasks for this project were:

- Develop an appropriate, activity-orientated curriculum
- Develop activities
- Create the lesson buildings
- Input Japanese into Minecraft

The project required some time and tools:

- Teacher preparation time: Over 100 hours
- Project duration: Ongoing
- Student time spent on project: Approximately 60 hours

- Minecraft environment: CraftBukkit
- Other tools: Google Docs; Language Cloud for homework, practice questions and videos; TeamSpeak for voice communication

Curriculum Development

Curriculum development is the most involved part of any educational project, whether it is hosted in a virtual world or not. Personally, it helped me to set a concrete goal. In the case of KM, this goal was to provide students with the necessary knowledge to pass the JLPT N5 test. This helped organize the progression of the course and even the design of the buildings and learning areas.

Occasionally, however, the game itself—a particular activity or plug-in—would inspire a lesson plan, and I would work backward from that.

Activity Development

I'll assume that you are aware of Minecraft's different game modes. **Table 9.1** highlights how these modes may be used for different language learning purposes. If such considerations are made, language teachers have immense freedom in activity design.

Table 9.1
Minecraft game modes and example activities

GAME MODE	ACTIVITY	LANGUAGE LEARNING OUTCOMES	LANGUAGE EXAMPLES
Creative	Building together (something to be used in future classes)	Giving and receiving Prepositions of place Conditionals	Shall we use wool for the walls? Put the table in front of the window, please. If we use black for the floor, this room will be too dark.

Table 9.1 continued
Minecraft game modes and example activities

GAME MODE	ACTIVITY	LANGUAGE LEARNING OUTCOMES	LANGUAGE EXAMPLES
Adventure	Cooperative "escape the room" challenge	Imperatives Question formation Imformation sharing	Jump now! Move three blocks left. What can you see? Is the creeper still there? I can see only one block. How about on your side?
Survival	Play together with teacher-defined objectives	Verb tenses	What are you doing? What did you do? What will you do next time?

Two-player co-op activities are a large feature on KM as a means to promote interaction. **Figures 9.1** and **9.2** show some of the KM world.

Figure 9.1
Guess who!

Created with the aid of Citizens 2, a plug-in for importing custom non-player characters (NPCs) into Minecraft, the activity in Figure 9.1 requires players to choose an NPC, then take turns asking their partner yes/no questions about the appearance of the NPCs to ascertain which NPC they have chosen. Typical dialogue might be:

Player A: Is it a man?

Player B: No. Does yours have a blue T-shirt?

Player A: Yes. Does yours have headphones?

Player B: Yes. Are you NPC1?

Player A: Yes.

Figure 9.2
Spot the
difference.

The activity shown in Figure 9.2 was designed to promote the use of the present continuous test (for example, "I am playing baseball" as opposed to "I play baseball"). The way this was achieved was by placing a number of NPCs in each of two houses. The NPCs were all engaged in a specific activity. However, in each house some of the NPCs are doing the same thing, whereas others are doing different things. Typical interaction might be:

Player A: What is Bob doing?

Player B: He is watching TV.

Player A: Oh! Here, Bob is eating breakfast.

Player B: OK, that is a difference. Is Rise swimming?

Player A: Yes.

Survival play has been used in a similar vein to promote the use of comparisons, question formation, and different tenses. But you should avoid merely assigning players the task of "playing in Survival mode." With pre-determined goals, students have something to work toward and something to talk about. Separating players into pairs has the additional bonus of getting groups to talk afterward about what they did. The activity starts as a pair-work activity, and then expands into a group discussion at the end.

Figure 9.3
Survival setup
for comparison activity.

The survival activity setup was to select a suitable selection of land, hide some resources and treasures, and then create a bedrock wall around the perimeter reaching from the bedrock level to the top of the map. After this, using the plug-in World Edit, it was possible to duplicate the whole area (**Figure 9.3**), creating multiple instances of the same arena for sets of pairs to play in. Next, we create objectives for the pairs. These objectives can be given a value of points for completing them ("XP" below) to encourage behavior in a certain direction. Objectives I created were:

- Find the nether star (100XP)
- Equip both players with iron armor (50XP)
- Find a diamond (50XP)
- Raise 20 sheep and cows

- Build a house with the following specifications (200XP):
  - Four windows
  - Bedroom
  - Table
  - Four chairs
  - Kitchen

After a certain amount of time has passed, stop the activity, split up the pairs, and partner with a player from another pair. Students can talk about what they did and didn't do, comparing their experiences.

There are a number of things that can help us design activities. JLPT N5 vocabulary and grammar requirements are not officially made available, but a number of resources are available that provide a fairly accurate outline. With reference to these resources, I designed activities that would promote using such vocabulary and grammar. Additionally, any beginner-level textbook can provide sufficient activities, and a number were referenced as part of this project.

Plug-ins themselves can be appropriated for use as language learning tools (**Figure 9.4**). One specific example of this is the plug-in Build My Thing. This is a multiplayer game, similar to the popular game Pictionary, in which one person is randomly selected to build an object based on a keyword whispered to them, and the remaining players have to guess what they are building by typing words into chat. One useful thing about this plug-in is that you can create the plug-in dictionary yourself; for example, we created a custom dictionary of Japanese words.

Figure 9.4
Appropriation of existing plug-ins.

The game can be used for a number of language learning objectives. By playing "as is," vocabulary can be learned, but if we overlook the "build and guess" play style, additional language-learning activities can be generated, such as:

- The person in the middle doesn't build but describes the item whispered to them. The remaining players guess.
- The person in the middle doesn't build but answers yes/no questions from the remaining players (essentially re-creating the famous 20 questions game).

Lesson Buildings and "JP Road"

Students who learn with us on KM do not have a pre-selected textbook. All lesson materials come from within the game itself and are designed by us. Initially, I used Google Docs to share words, phrases, grammar tips, and lesson plans. The problem with this was that it was awkward going from Google Docs to the game, and I had a predisposition to host as much material as I could in the game world itself. In other words, I wanted to have to rely on external tools as little as possible. I now realize that other tools, such as Google Docs, have a purpose in KM for collaborative writing and reading lessons. From this notion, the development of a university building, or "learning zone," emerged. The problem was that the university would have to be huge to house all the material I wanted to cover. A modular design was instead favored and eventually chosen. Essentially, lessons would be housed in buildings known as the JP buildings, and these buildings would be in a row. This row of buildings was thus called JP Road.

Each floor of the JP buildings (**Figure 9.5**) represents a lesson.

Each building is arbitrarily devided into a certain number of floors, and the whole course is contained within ten buildings: JP1 through JP10. In each room, there are typically new words, grammar, and activities (**Figures 9.6** through **9.8**).

Figure 9.5
Original concept
design for the
JP buildings.

Figure 9.6
New words.

Figure 9.7
Grammar.

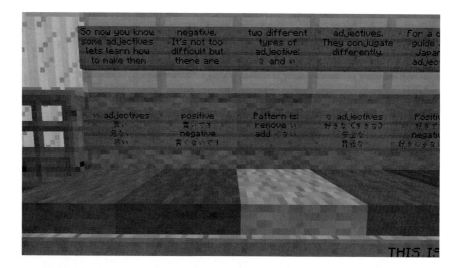

Figure 9.8
Activities.

The JP Road design (**Figure 9.9**) was the most logical way of having all learning material in the same place, and there was no problem when only the first few buildings were complete. But as more and more buildings became filled with signs, the frame rate for most players (even those with high-spec PCs) dropped dramatically when they tried to navigate the area. This was disastrous for the road system and led to the developent of a new system. This was initially very frustrating, but now

I am happy that this problem arose, because the evolution from JP Road to JP area has been a very positive experience.

Figure 9.9
Finished version of JP Road.

The current state of the learning area is shown in **Figures 9.10** and **9.11**. Buildings stands 15 chunks apart to ensure that only one building is ever rendered at a time. Activities surrounding each building are relevant to the learning material inside.

Note
I am aware that people can increase the default number of chunks that can be seen, but in general people are limited to about 12 chunks.

Figure 9.10
The JP8 building and learning activities.

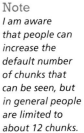

Figure 9.11
Aerial view of
the JP area.

Japanese Input

Japanese input—or, more importantly, Unicode input—is not supported in Minecraft by default, but this limitation can be surmounted with additional plug-ins.

- Intellinput is a mod for the client-side version of Minecraft. It allows players to input Japanese directly into the chat box.

- Lunachat is a fantastic server-side plug-in that takes users' text, sends it to Google (not sure of the details), and brings back the Japanese characters for that text. The Japanese text is then shown in the chat box. The raw input is shown after the Japanese text. **Figure 9.12** shows how this looks in the game.

Figure 9.12
Chat box.

[E] [Teacher]Cheapshot: これは日本語です (korehanihongodesu)

- Internet relay chat (IRC) allows messages as text. It is possible to add an IRC channel to your server with CraftIRC. With an IRC, it is possible to type directly into the Minecraft chat channel from the external IRC channel. This also doubles as a good way to monitor activities on the server and participate in discussions even when you are not able to log in to the game directly.

Getting Started

Unlike MinecraftEdu, which is very popular among teachers for its security and teacher-friendly controls, Bukkit has no inherent protection against griefing—the act of maliciously destroying other players' builds or stealing items. I highly recommend the following three plug-ins to prevent such griefing:

- World Guard allows you to protect important builds so that they will not be destroyed by others. Additionally, it allows you to define the game mode for specific areas.

- Group Manager. With this, you can create a number of player groups whose permissions are customizable. The default groups are admin, moderator, builder, and guest. You can also add groups to World Guard areas, giving build access to only certain members.

- Essentials features a host of useful commands, such as /warp, /teleport, /gamemode, and /seen. You can grant permission to use these commands on a per-player or per-group basis if using Group Manager.

I also recommend these plug-ins:

- Dynmap is an interactive, online map of the game world. Very useful for seeing where everyone is building and to locate specific warps.

- Variable Triggers is a plug-in we rely on a lot at KM. It has a whole range of uses, but the one I use most is to cause signs in the game to whisper a URL to players when clicked.

- Citizens 2 and Denizens. We use these for the creation of interactive NPC characters.

Completing the Tasks

The Japanese course that I teach has been a long time in creation from the humble (read: shabby) buildings and scattered activities of the first implementation to the simple, aesthetically pleasing and practical area that it is now. This came about through trial and error, player feedback, and player contributions, so it is not easy for me to provide a step-by-step guide to creating a similar server. Although I can offer the following dos and don'ts.

1. Start with a concrete objective.
2. Take inspiration from lessons you already teach outside Minecraft.
3. Make use of all game modes.
4. Focus on creating a need to be in Minecraft. If the activity can be done without it, it is probably better not to use Minecraft.
5. Prioritize pair or small-group work to maximize individual output.
6. Create small goals within a larger, more holistic activity to focus student interaction from moment to moment.

In my opinion, the KM server will never be complete. This is not to say that it is an unfinished project but rather that it is constantly evolving, with new material always being added. At this point, I have a team working on building a city that will be used as the arena for an immersive roleplay-based curriculum. In other words, they have an airport, a train station, restaurants and other common shops, and a residential area. Each area has a specific roleplay activity in mind. We are working on a survival games map to pit player versus player.

Reflection and Assessment

This project has been a labor of love for well over a year, and although a number of activities could be re-created to be more engaging or Minecraft specific, I am very happy with the way the project has turned out. Feedback from students is generally positive, and the experience they are getting is the one that I envisioned: social learning with an emphasis on speaking and listening in a "real classroom in an unreal world." Or as another student described it, "textbook content without a textbook."

Project Future

One thing that I haven't been spending too much time on is how to teach kanji (the Chinese characters used in Japanese). I personally used a system called "Remembering the Kanji," by James Heisig. A number of free online resources for studying kanji use this method, and a number of alternatives systematically teach kanji. Because of the low-resolution graphics of Minecraft, it is hard enough writing the roman alphabet using Minecraft blocks, let alone an incredibly intricate character such as "離".

We have a weekly activity on the server called "Let's Play in Japanese." As the name suggests, we play games together in Japanese. The class is not formal, and vocabulary and grammar are kept to a minimum so that we can focus on actually playing. We've mainly focused on Minecraft until now, but we are experimenting with other multiplayer games, such as Rust, League of Legends, and a Garry's Mod game called DarkRP. Player suggestions are also welcome. In a sense, the KM server hosts a formal, guided course in Japanese, and then we apply this knowledge to play other games together (including Minecraft).

Finally, I think the KM model is transferable for other languages. There is of course a need for language-specific buildings (such as those to explain the use of le, la, and l' in French, pluralization rules in English, and more), but most activities are very much transferable. So if any readers would like to teach another language with us, please get in touch!

Resources

Listed here are programs and tools that can assist with the Kotoba Miners activity:

- Kotoba Miners official homepage: www.kotobaminers.org

  This is where you can find the address to join our server, as well as discuss language learning with other students on the forums.

- Kotoba Miners blog: http://blog.kotobaminers.org

  Content that is related to the Kotoba Miners project, Japan, and language learning.

- Language Cloud: https://languagecloud.co/

  I use this to create homework exersices for my students. It is very easy to create curriculum content, and it features a plethora of question types, such as fill-the-gap, multiple choice, written answer, matching, and so on.

- Planet Minecraft: www.planetminecraft.com

    Very useful for getting large builds to import into your server. A lot of content here is freely available to use, but it is always a good idea to ask the creators if you can use their content.

- Bukkit: http://bukkit.org/

    This website hosts the craftbukkit server files and all the plug-ins mentioned in this chapter.

- Additonal resources that have been mentioned in previous chapters include:

    - Minecraft homepage
    - Minecraft wiki
    - Google Drive

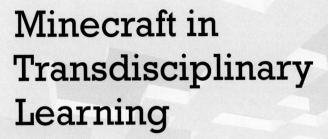

Minecraft in Transdisciplinary Learning

Thousands of schools worldwide use the International Baccaulaureate (IB) framework. Included in this four-program continuum is the the Primary Years Program (PYP); its school year is composed of six transdisciplinary units of inquiry, which usually, last six weeks each (the time frame changes from school to school and from unit to unit). It was during the "How We Organize Ourselves" unit that we embarked on integrating Minecraft into my school.

I have to thank the third grade teachers I have worked with over the past two years for their adaptability, flexibility, and vision in undertaking and completing this project. As the technology coach in my school, I often get the plaudits for introducing Minecraft, but the classroom teachers are the ones who ensure student learning is always taking place. A special thanks goes out to Sharyn Skrtic, Anjana Dayal, and Shanez Cabraal for the use of their students' work.

Colin Gallagher

I've been working at the ISS International School for three years. Before that I worked in Hong Kong and Germany. One of my hobbies outside school is video gaming—using Minecraft in education is something I didn't need much encouragement to pursue.

I've interviewed over 20 teachers so far in my Minechat YouTube series, but I've never interviewed my colleagues about our Minecraft project. I need to make that happen soon!

Project Summary

In the third grade, the central idea of the "How We Organize Ourselves" unit is "Communities can function because of the systems within them." It is with that statement that we started planning and executing a four- to five-week project using Minecraft as a focal tool. Each third grade class creates its own world and works together to create a town or city that incoporates the class's idea of what systems are essential (and which ones are inessential but nice to have) in a functioning community.

At the start of the unit of inquiry, students embark on many learning engagements to assess prior knowledge before Minecraft is even mentioned (this worked the first year, but the second year the students had heard on the playground grapevine what was coming up). An example of one of these experiences is examining mystery bags containing random systems (with pieces missing) to get the students inquiring what it might be, how it might work, and why it doesn't work now.

Throughout the unit of inquiry, students investigate systems in school, systems at home, the postal system, procedural writing describing the process of a system, and human needs and wants. It's this last investigation that leads to the question of which systems in a community are essential for human needs and which systems exist because of human wants.

Project Goals

During the years before Minecraft existed, a project in this unit of inquiry would have taken the form of cardboard and sticky tape (not that there's anything wrong with that). We thought that by using Minecraft, the students would be able to immerse themselves in their 3D community and see their systems better, to be able to walk around and inside and between systems. That is powerful.

In essense, our goal for using Minecraft is to transform what the students create into something that is otherwise impossible to achieve. We envision that some students, who may not learn something from seeing their community on paper or made with cardboard, will be more engaged with a digital model of their community.

We also know that digital citizenship (which was not part of the unit of inquiry planner) plays a big part, and we welcome this gladly. This is the first time students have to collaborate and communicate effectively in a digital realm. They have to learn trust and teamwork.

Learning Objectives

There are three lines of inquiry that clarify the central idea and define the scope of the inquiry:

- The purpose of systems (function)
- The connection between systems (connection)
- The effect these systems have on a community (causation)

The teacher questions that frame the inquiry and promote conceptual development are the following:

- What is a system?
- What systems do communities rely on?
- What would happen if systems break down?
- How are different systems interconnected?

In between their time on Minecraft, the students are directed and prompted to think along, and beyond, the lines of inquiry. They take part in learning engagements that cross subject borders (transdisciplinary): math (coordinates), literacy (procedural writing), and social studies (people's needs and wants).

A set of skills we want our students to acquire and apply are what the IB calls transdisciplinary skills:

- Social skills: accepting responsibility, cooperating, group decision making
- Self-management skills: spatial awareness, organization, time management
- Thinking skills: application

Through using Minecraft, social skills are magnified and have a more authentic and relevant twist. Our students are increasingly active online. If we can help our third grade students work effectively with others in a digital environment, where it is much harder to communicate effectively, we can give them a huge step forward in their future careers.

Self-management skills also take on a more digital slant in Minecraft. Poor spatial awareness is a common ailment that falls upon many

Minecraft players. It is vital for our students to develop organization and time management skills, because we have a strict plan and timeline to follow.

The IB has developed the IB Learner Profile, which is a set of attributes to inspire and motivate students. In this unit of inquiry, we identified the following attributes to highlight:

- Caring
- Communicators
- Open-minded

These attributes are reflected upon throughout our unit of inquiry, whether it is outside Minecaft, interviewing members of their community or working together effectively in Minecraft.

Another essential element of the PYP are the personal attitudes to raise awareness of and build an appreciation of. We provided opportunities for our students to develop the following attititudes:

- Cooperation
- Tolerance

When working with a group of people in Minecraft, you need cooperation and tolerance. Being sensitive to other students' differences and abilities and being part of an effective collaborative group of students is very important to develop and focus on.

Organizing the Project

The project requires some prepartaion in terms of tools and time. Here are some tools and timeframes that are needed for the project:

- Teacher preparation time: Five or six hours
- Project duration: Four to five weeks
- Student classroom time spent on project: Roughly 800 minutes in Minecraft creating their community
- Minecraft environment: Minecraft and MinecraftEdu
- Other tools: Large sheets of paper, Google Apps, QuickTime Player (to create video walkthroughs)

Outside Minecraft

As students learn about systems and systems within communities, they strengthen their vocabulary and awareness of human wants and needs in a community (**Figures 10.1** and **10.2**).

Figure 10.1
Students brain-storm which systems appear in working communities.

Figure 10.2
Students deter-
mine which
things are needs
and which
are wants.

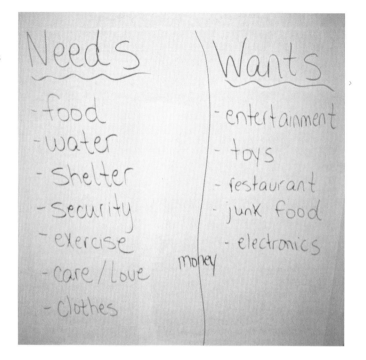

Before starting any work using Minecraft, each class develops a huge plan on a big sheet of paper. Positions are discussed and roles are assigned. Some students, for example, are in charge of transport and some in charge of dwellings, but all students know their roles and know they must stick to the plan that the class collectively comes up with.

After establishing the initial plan (which can be altered by mutual agree-ment of the whole class), they start transforming their paper plan into Minecraft (**Figures 10.3** through **10.6**).

The paper plans differ somewhat between classes, and that is perfectly fine.

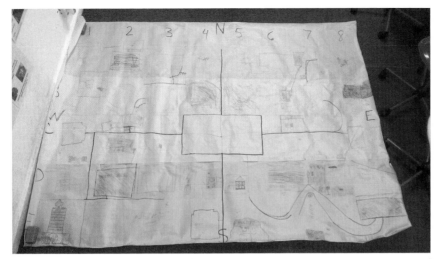

Figure 10.3
Although cumbersome, the size of the maps is conducive to group planning.

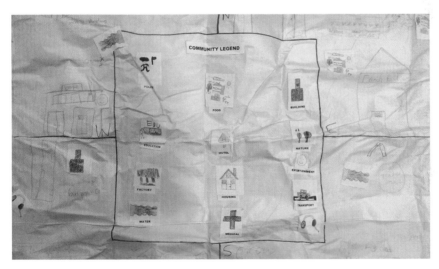

Figure 10.4
I like the way various classes organize the map differently. This class created a legend, which made the map neater.

Figure 10.5
This class used
pieces of paper
to represent
systems in the
community.

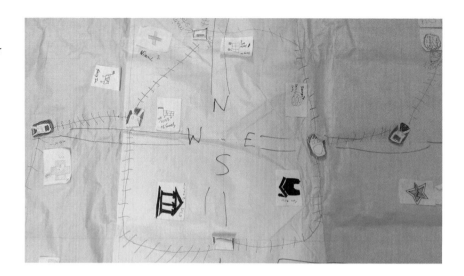

Figure 10.6
A closeup of
a student's
meticulous plan-
ning. The MRT
is the Singapore
metro system.

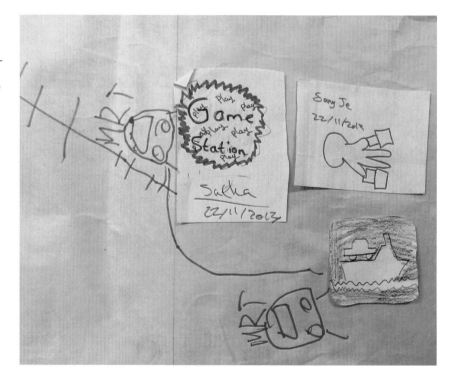

Inside Minecraft

The nuts and bolts of the Minecraft setup for our project needed a number of weeks for planning. That was one of the last times I used an outside host with regular old Minecraft, and it took a bit of preparation (I now use MinecraftEdu). I used the Minecraft admin tool McMyAdmin because it was what my host used.

The first year, I used a flat map, which seemed ideal. It was deep enough for any underground train system that a student deemed a necessary system for the community. I did not make any changes to the maps. The downside was that students had no focal point or sense of direction once inside. So I created a central square with four roads extending in four directions, labeled north, south, east, and west. Now students wouldn't get lost so easily and could look at their paper plan to know exactly which direction to start building.

I used the settings shown in **Figure 10.7** for the world.

Figure 10.7
As you can tell from the settings, I wanted nothing to distract from the task of building. We allowed animals only after students made a good case for them.

The plug-ins I installed were mainly to stop any sort of unwanted destruction from happening (**Figure 10.8**). In the first year of this project, we had a quite a few moments of destruction, and although we saw them as learning moments, we had a tight schedule to keep and couldn't keep rectifying massive holes in the ground and fires that burned as far as the eye could see. We came up with a set of rules for our third grade class worlds that covers respect and responsibility (see "Getting Started").

Figure 10.8
Most of these plug-ins are self-explanatory, but KickFas disables flint and steel (guess why), and CoreProtect gives me (or anyone I set as the moderator of the Minecraft world) the ability to see who removes or places blocks.

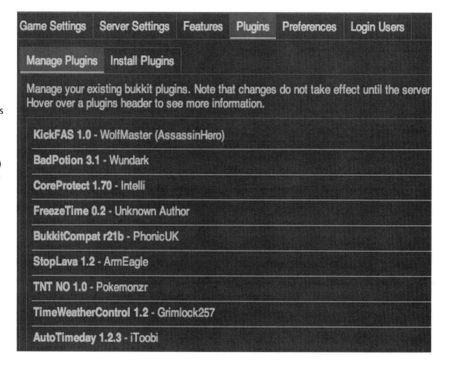

The management of plug-ins is not easy, because as Minecraft updates, plug-ins can go out of date and stop. For this reason, the next time I set up Minecraft, I will be switching to MinecraftEdu for the ease of management of each world.

So that was it, the Minecraft worlds were ready—the maps were made, the plug-ins installed, and the world configuration set. We were ready for the students!

Getting Started

In the first session together in the project, the students have their massive paper plan already started and spread out on the floor to check and double-check. They continue to use it throughout the four to five weeks of the project. Before the students use Minecraft, I conduct a ten-minute presentation, during which they can ask questions. The teachers have drilled into them that the Minecraft we work in at school has different goals and rules than the Minecraft they might play at home (**Figure 10.9**).

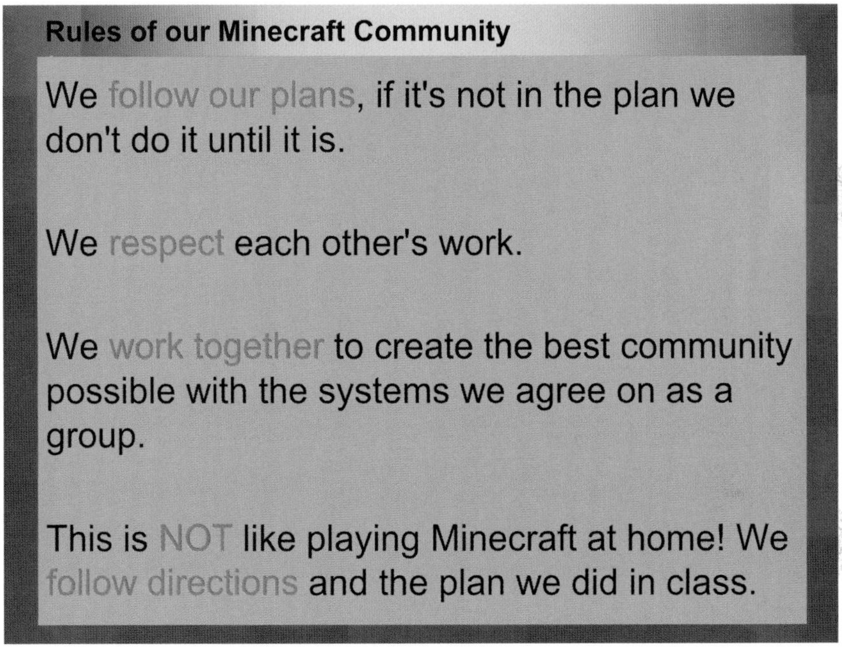

Rules of our Minecraft Community

We follow our plans, if it's not in the plan we don't do it until it is.

We respect each other's work.

We work together to create the best community possible with the systems we agree on as a group.

This is NOT like playing Minecraft at home! We follow directions and the plan we did in class.

Figure 10.9
We want the rules to be simple yet effective and to be as positively worded as possible. We reiterate the difference between Minecraft at school and home.

The presentation runs through the basics of Minecraft: how to gain access to the multiplayer world and how the mouse and keyboard control every move. A lot of students have Minecraft PE on their iPads, which is quite different to control than the full-blown version on a Mac or PC. We also have a laminated slide that illustrates the controls for students who find them hard to remember. That works very well (**Figures 10.10** through **10.12**).

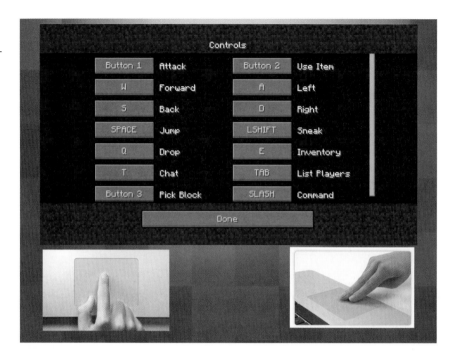

Figure 10.10
The basics of moving in Minecraft. This is invaluable for some students. We need to add how right-click works on a Macbook Pro.

Figure 10.11
Another tricky part when starting with Minecraft is how to get the blocks you want.

With the first and second grade classes using Minecraft, we spend two classes learning the controls and going through the tutorial world in MinecraftEdu. With the third grade classes, we dive straight in. For students who find using the mouse and keyboard controls difficult, we use a number of methods to help: we physically place their hands on the mouse and keyboard and model how you move and build, and we use peer assistance in which more-proficient students help struggling class-mates (and give better tips than the teachers in many situations).

The major focus of the teachers is to make sure the plan is being fol-lowed. Throughout the project, we have students stop what they are building and identify on the paper plan the corresponding point in the project where they are in Minecraft. We confirm together that they are building where they should be building. I see students constantly check-ing the paper map to ensure they are at the correct coordinates before they start constructing. We see two of the self-management skills we want them to develop in those instances: spatial awareness and organi-zation (**Figure 10.13**).

So getting started with this project is a culmination of a lot of tuning-in activities with the classroom teachers regarding systems and systems in communities, a lot of prep work in making the Minecraft worlds ready, and an enthusiastic set of students eager to transform their paper plan and their developing ideas into a fully immersive 3D world.

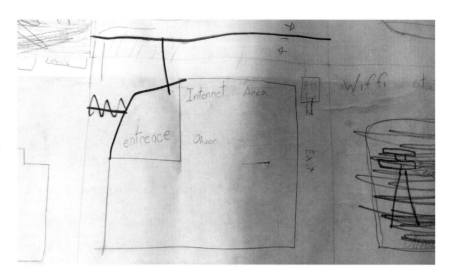

Figure 10.13
You can see in this close-up of one of our paper maps that changes and mistakes were corrected as we went along. We encourage using pencils from time to time.

Completing the Tasks

After setting our expectations and getting students comfortable with the controls, it is full steam ahead for the students and their blossoming community. This is an untraditional project in the sense that we don't set out to do Minecraft every day at 9:00 a.m. Teachers reserve media lab time slots in advance for however much time they need. It is a flexible but well organized project with clearly defined goals for the students.

I define a "task" in this project as a structure or building that a student has to complete next in their job list. Completing tasks is a regular occurence and very dynamic for our students. Everyone has tasks that are identified on the paper plan. Students know their roles (**Figure 10.14**).

If we as teachers see that the student in charge of transportation is lagging behind, we have another student who may be ahead of schedule help with the roads or underground tunnels for trains. If we see a student undertaking a monumentously ambitious building project akin to the Burj Dubai, we discuss with the student how to manage the scope of the task given the timeframe of the project.

Figure 10.14
Certain students are in charge of the transportation systems. Minecraft makes it easy to create train lines, which is good because Singapore has an excellent system of underground transportation.

Completing tasks looks different for every student (**Figures 10.15** through **10.17**).

Figure 10.15
A student contemplates his next move as he types in a sign above a building. Signs play an important role in figuring out the function of each building.

Figure 10.16
The transferring of the north-south-east-west coordinates into our Minecraft map. Here, a student builds an office building not unlike the ones you see around Singapore.

Figure 10.17
A community in progress. Although it's a little messy-looking from above (isn't every city?), you could easily walk to the paper map, point at something, and tell a student to show you that building in the Minecraft world.

Reflection and Assessment

Minecraft enables students to vizualize systems within communities in a way not possible before, allowing them to walk through their systems. It has transformed the way we deliver this unit of inquiry. Having said that, it isn't the only tool of learning, but it certainly is one that enhances students' perception of what they have learned and adds value to the learning process. It helps students conceptualize how systems interact in a community. It helps students feel like part of a community while learning about communities. It helps our students develop a set of transdisciplinary skills while fully immersed in a digital world.

Students are assessed in three ways: two formative assessments and one summative assessment. These assessments give teachers the opportunity to provide ongoing feedback to the students in order for them to further develop their understanding of the central idea throughout the unit of inquiry.

- **Formative:** Students complete a checklist every time they enter Minecraft. Teachers use the checklist to assess the development of a student's transdisciplinary skills throughout the project, and teachers can track how the student feels about the work accomplished (**Table 10.1**). Dated entries by students help them reflect on how efficiently they worked that day and help teachers understand which transdisciplinary skills are progressing and which are not.

Table 10.1
Self-Reflection Checklist

STUDENT SELF-REFLECTION CHECKLIST—SYSTEMS IN A COMMUNITY

(4–Above expectations; 3–Meeting expectations;
2–Approaching expectations; 1–Experiencing difficulties)

	NOV 25	NOV 26	DEC 2	DEC 3	DEC 6
Did I ask others to share space, knowledge, ideas?	3	3	3	2	4
Did I stick to the plan?	4	4	4	4	4
Did I talk to others before making decisions?	3	3	3	4	4
Am I using NSWE (directions) to place things?	4	4	4	4	3
Did I watch how much time I spent on one thing?	3	3	3	4	4
Did I work together when something went wrong?	NA	NA	3	NA	NA

- **Formative:** Students self-assess their work as a community on another rubric. They complete this rubric three or four times during the project. Teachers use this rubric to determine how the overall project is coming along from the students' perspective (**Table 10.2**).

- **Summative:** When the community is finished, the students are assesssed on the walkthrough videos they created to show their final work. Some students are guided by a script, prepared by the teachers, that prompts them to show what we want them to show (**Figure 10.18**).

Table 10.2
Rubric focused on the students' work as a community

CRITERIA	EXCEEDING EXPECTATIONS	MEETING EXPECTATIONS	APPROACHING EXPECTATIONS	EXPERIENCING DIFFICULTIES
Planning	Minecraft model followed blueprints exactly with appropriate changes made on blueprints first.	Minecraft model mostly followed blueprint.	Minecraft model followed some of the blueprint.	Minecraft model showed no relation to blueprint plan.
Needs and Wants	Systems were created insightfully and thoughtfully based on needs and wants of a community.	Systems were created based on needs and wants of a community.	Some systems were created based on needs and wants of a community.	Very few systems were created based on needs and wants of a community.
Design	Systems were attractive, detailed, and thoughtfully located with a purpose.	The systems were located thoughtfully in the community with a purpose.	Most of the systems were located thoughtfully with a purpose.	Some systems were missing or placed without thought.
Cooperation	Cooperation and communication were strong. Disagreements were handled responsibly.	Class worked cooperatively together with one or two disagreements.	Disagreements delayed progress of community.	Community lacks systems or completion due to arguments.

›CHOOSE ONE
(I will start recording with me:
-in the sky looking down on community
-on the ground, near something I built)

START TALKING
Hello, my name is _____ or in Minecraft you can
call me _____.
Welcome to _____, our G3 Community.

I was responsible for _____.

I also helped _____.

This is one of my structures, it is _____.

FUNCTION: How does it work?
_____
_____

CONNECTION: What is it connected to?
_____
_____

CAUSATION: Why is it like this, what would happen if we
didn't have it?
_____
_____
_____

These are the Transdisciplinary skills I applied when I was
building in Minecraft. (explain how)

Figure 10.18
The prompts
steer students to
share their learn-
ing aligned with
the three key
concepts (func-
tion, connection,
and causation)
and the transdis-
ciplinary skills.

Sharing the Project

Students use Google Sites as portfolios in our school, and as the project progresses, students embed their self-assessment checklists and rubrics. Along with that, each of our classrooms has a blog on which students can show work to the outside world (**Figure 10.19**). The most powerful result is that students from other schools can see what our students are doing, ask questions, and get ideas about their own projects (**Figure 10.20**).

Figure 10.19 One of the many student posts on the classroom blog.

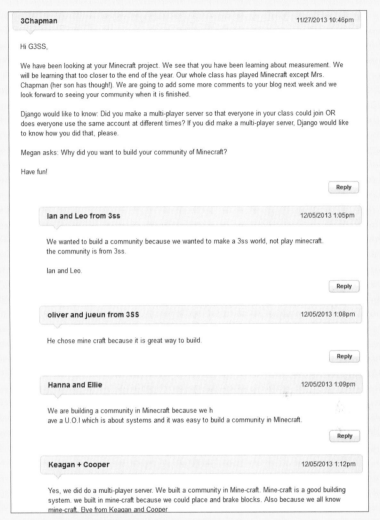

Figure 10.20 Another school inquires about our Minecraft project, and our students respond.

Project Future

You're not in the right job if you're not constantly figuring out how to improve your lessons or the projects you create for your students. This project is no exception. As mentioned, I added the central square and directions after the first year. Next year, I will likely create a grid with a coordinate name along with the directions so that we have spaces laid out more formally, and so the paper plan and Minecraft world will synchronize more efficiently.

One of the major changes I will undertake is the switch to MinecraftEdu, which will provide more control over the worlds and will allow creating just one map and copying the map to each classroom world. I also will not have to worry about plug-ins not being up to date, as I do on our regular Minecraft server.

In an international school, teachers move around regularly, so we will most likely have new teachers every one or two years. With the introduction of Minecraft to the first and second grade classes in our school, we hope that we are cultivating a learning environment that sees Minecraft as a tool for learning and teaching and not just for slaying zombies and creepers.

Resources

Listed here are programs and tools that can assist with the Minecraft community and systems activity:

- Dan's beautiful flat map: http://tinyurl.com/danflatmap
- International Baccalaureate curriculum: www.ibo.org
- My and Sharyn Skrtic's presentation on our project after the first year: http://goo.gl/uRiVoN

Minecraft and Special Educational Needs

It was in April 2014 that I first talked with André in his Minecraft world. It was apparent that he was seeking ways for his students with differing educational needs to have positive, meaningful learning moments with Minecraft. There has been a lot of press recently about how Minecraft can help with educational needs; it's an interesting time to determine what aspects of Minecraft can help students.

Project Summary

Our school's Minecraft project, Civcraft, evolved from the idea of combining Minecraft game mechanics with the game Civilization. The idea was to use Minecraft to simulate historical periods, where students would experience the advances of a civilization by playing in Minecraft. The intent was to create and use this one-time project to determine the value that such a game could have on instruction and if it was valuable enough to invest further development time.

The gameplay was similar to Minecraft, but when certain premises and rules were set up, students were allowed to experience life in the Mesolithic period through their avatar.

André Chercka

I began exploring the potentials of digital games in 2010, after teaching for 10 years in the Danish school system. My first attempt was using Battlefield 2 in math class, and soon afterward a student introduced me to Minecraft. Since then I have been exploring the many possibilities of the game with my students and have also made an effort to document and share my experiences. Presently I am the workshop teacher at the Gameworkshop at Glostrup Albertslund Production High School, where our core production at this workshop is to create Minecraft games for educational purposes.

Civcraft was an elective course that was held once weekly for 90 minutes over a period of three months. The students were 14 young men from 17 to 20 years old. All had different learning challenges, and most had either an ADHD or Asperger's diagnosis.

The sessions were organized with an instructional period of 15 minutes in which a summary of the session was presented, and the remaining hour and 15 minutes were spent playing.

Since many learning-challenged students have difficulty absorbing information presented verbally, the content and rules of the game were presented in the game. This gave students an immersive experience when introduced to the game (**Figure 11.1**), and at the same time allowed them to gain more understanding by seeing, reading, and interacting with content.

After this introduction, students spawned into a 2000x2000-block terrain (**Figure 11.2**), where they were given assignments to solve collaboratively and in pairs.

A part of making this course accessible to my students was making it as a game. The game provided a structure for them to work in, and it provided a well-known platform from which they could develop new competencies.

Figure 11.1
The lobby, where students were introduced to the game.

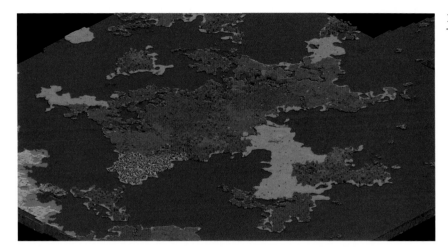

Figure 11.2
The game terrain.

Project Goals

Civcraft was an untried game idea. The project was to explore whether or not such an idea was worth expanding and developing—would it work?

The idea of letting students experience life in the Stone Age through Minecraft from a first-person perspective was also something new. So the virtual, physical, and organizational designs were all experiments, being adjusted and tweaked throughout the course.

Our school works with individualized learning plans, so the goal of teaching a specific curriculum was not central for this project. Most of the students did not have much knowledge of the historical content we would be covering. Acquiring knowledge through a more traditional approach was a challenge for them. Civcraft was intended to make content that did not have a direct appeal to a group of students accessible to them, by presenting it in an immersive, informal context.

The group of students I was working with were ideal subjects with whom to conduct this test. A number of the students had very short concentration spans, which meant that when planning the sessions, information would have to be conveyed visually and through play (**Figure 11.3**) rather than by verbal instruction or text. Another consideration was that information about gameplay had to be presented on a need-to-know basis to accommodate the needs of students with short-term memory loss.

Figure 11.3
The materials allowed for building the first settlement.

In reality, preparing a lesson with these features in mind are some of the components of good game design. It might sound counter to teaching philosophies, but if students are required to think too much about every move they make, the flow of the game is disrupted and thereby the immersive effect is lost.

Learning Objectives

A central premise to designing this course was that the students did not come to learn about history, but to play. Although their individualized learning plans did not require them to master history in any degree, I saw it as a part of their general education and something that would broaden their horizons.

The learning objectives were divided into three areas:

- Training the ability to work collaboratively (**Figure 11.4**)
  - Problem-solving and decision-making
  - Communicating and organizing
  - Constructing and sharing information
  - Resolving conflicts

- Gaining historical knowledge about life in the Stone Age:
  - The end of the Ice Age and the first people migrating to Danish soil
  - Living in the Stone Age
  - Agriculture, monuments, and settlements
- Testing Civcraft as a game concept:
  - Providing constructive feedback regarding gameplay, assignments, and rewards
  - Reflecting on game mechanics and providing students an opportunity to express these thoughts in precise language

Figure 11.4
Preparing for the night: an exercise in collaboration.

For the students, playing Civcraft felt most like a game. Learning historical facts came through mastering the gameplay and completing assignments throughout the game.

Learning became a byproduct of play rather than a result of explicit instruction. The historical content in the game was based on materials for the fourth grade, and Civcraft was designed with this user group in mind. Nevertheless, my group of 17- to 20-year-olds delved into the game with no reservations.

Organizing the Project

In creating the structure for this game, I divided it into levels, and new technologies were introduced through each assignment. When assignments were completed, students received the apropriate reward and moved on to the next.

Creating the Design

As with any game design, creating a concept and following through on all the details became time consuming. The first challenge was how to make the game mechanics work and how I could import concepts from Civilization into Minecraft. In the research phase, I spent all my time looking at tech trees from Civilization to get an idea of which technologies I could bring to life in Minecraft. Tech trees in Civilization provide a chronological overview of all the technologies throughout the game.

I then began organizing the technologies of the ages in a spreadsheet, aligning elements of Minecraft with technologies from Civilization. **Table 11.1** shows some of the technologies from history, abilities made possible by the technologies, and how they align with gameplay abilities.

Table 11.1
Excerpts from technology alignment charts

CIVILIZATION TECHNOLOGY	BUILDINGS AND INVENTORY ALLOWED WHEN DISCOVERED	GAMEPLAY NECESSARY TO DISCOVER THE TECHNOLOGY
Mining	Torch, cobblestone pickaxe, axe, sword (wooden and stone)	Find wood, coal, stone
Craftsmanship	Wood, sticks, wooden plank, crafting table, chest, wooden axe, wooden pickaxe, ladder, beds, bowls	Decide on a location for a first settlement (chieftain's responsibility)
Hunting	Wooden and stone sword, leather armor	Go hunting for pig, cow and chicken
Religion	Temple, shrine, obelisk, Stonehenge	Build a monument for religious ceremonies

For example, archery was discovered when you created a bow and arrow, and craftsmanship was discovered when a shelter was built.

As the tribes became more advanced, they in turn were allowed to use more materials. Because of this altered gameplay, students had to progress through a number of assignments before they could start using iron.

This presented me with a challenge that would make the game either fail or succeed: Would students accept these restrictions, or would they succumb to the mechanics of regular survival Minecraft? It would definitely happen if I did not create an alternative game mechanic to engage the students or prevent them from playing through the routines of Survival Minecraft.

Here is where Minecraft culture lends itself well to education: Players define their own rules and premises. This culture allows educators and students to approach Minecraft as a broader learning platform and not just as a game. In such a setting, the teacher becomes a game maker, setting rules and boundaries but still leading from behind.

After creating the connection between the technology advances of Civilization and Minecraft, the next step was to define challenges and rewards. The historical content that I wished to cover had to be embedded within these challenges, while following some of the basic routines of survival gameplay.

As an example, the first challenge was to establish leadership in a tribe. This was connected to the ability of creating fire in Minecraft. The first player in a tribe to create a torch became the chieftain of that tribe. This session of play, which lasted about 10 minutes, became an opportunity for me to spark a discussion about power structures in a tribe and the necessity of fire for survival.

Another example where Minecraft gameplay brilliantly illustrated life in the Stone Age was a challenge called "man's best friend." (**Figure 11.5**). Students were to tame a wolf with a bone and use it both as protection and for hunting. This session of play illustrated the important advancement of domestication and how it affected everyday life.

Figure 11.5
Man's best
friend: Here
students tamed
wolves and used
them for hunting
and protection.

Designing the Lobby

The lobby area was where students entered the game. It is best described as a combination of a virtual museum and a game guide. Here, students were introduced to the concept and rules of the game, given the historical background of the period, and experienced the designs of the structures they were to build (**Figure 11.6**).

Figure 11.6
Level 3 presents
agriculture and
housing in the
Stone Age.

In preparation, each level took approximately two hours for me to build, and using the building tools in MinecraftEdu made this very efficient. What took the longest time was adapting texts for the text blocks and designing the layout of the level. Once these were in place, the actual building did not take much time.

The lobby was divided into five levels, each covering a certain area of content. A level comprised two to five different assignments (**Table 11.2**). My plan was that a level was to be played through every class session, which lasted 90 minutes.

Table 11.2
Overview of assignments in level 2

ASSIGNMENT	OBJECTIVES	REWARD
The hunt	Go on a hunt using a bow and arrow and a fishing rod.	Bones
Man's best friend	Find and tame a wolf. Use it for hunting and protection.	Iron ore
The dugout canoe	Go exploring in your boats.	Discover the land and find rewards
Nomad life	Move your settlement to a new location.	Seeds

The project required some time and tools:

- Teacher preparation time: Approximately 30 minutes per 90-minute class session
- Project duration: 10 sessions over 3 months
- Student time spent on project: Approximately 90 minutes per session
- Minecraft environment: MinecraftEdu
- Other tools: Google Docs, interactive whiteboard (to present game environment and prepare the class before logging in)

Getting Started

After a brief presentation of the first session, students were allowed to log in and await further instruction in the lobby. Since most of my students were not able to grasp too much information at once, I did not base the lesson on them remembering everything I showed them.

The most important message that they needed to understand was that they were in the Stone Age, and that successful gameplay was dependent on them being in character. I was surprised, though, that most students took the time to read the texts I had placed in the lobby, which mostly described the historical setting we were playing in.

Initially, I had planned the game to be played in Survival mode, but after the first session, I realized that students were becoming sidetracked by dealing with hostile mobs while completing the assignments. Instead, I disabled monsters and only enabled them when it became relevant to an assignment, or to vary the gameplay.

After spawning into the game terrain, all they had to do was follow the assignments given. I had not foreseen that students would insist on optimizing their game, as if they were in competition with the other tribe. They did this by communicating verbally across the workshop, coordinating their work and sharing information.

Even though I had not consciously created this game mechanic, it made students pursue the goals I set throughout the game. In retrospect, I could have put this to much better use by letting the competition animate students to collaborate more.

Session Management

The 14 students were divided into two "tribes," and each tribe was placed in separate rooms. The first challenges required all players in a tribe to act together and come to agreement about how they would work; that is, coordinating who would build, hunt, and collect resources. Later on, I encountered the challenge of how to reward fairly when certain individuals or groups of players produced good work. I found that I needed to subdivide the tribes into groups of two and three, letting them collaborate in completing their assignments. In this way, I could inspect their work when they finished an assignment and reward accordingly.

There were also issues of conflict during play, where students either didn't collaborate or engaged in antisocial behavior. One area of conflict was when students embarked on side projects and did not focus on the actual assignments. And there was griefing: In one tribe two students formed an alliance in which they griefed and did not contribute to the tribe's work.

To turn this conflict into something constructive, I challenged students to discuss what happened to tribe members who did not work for the common good of the family. The consequences in the game were logical because there was a sense of urgency surrounding the challenges that they met. Everyone agreed that the non-contributors could either be excluded from the tribe or forced to start again on their own.

I find it very interesting that a part of the engaging experience in playing through a certain role lets students experience the tensions that a tribe might face when confronted with such conflicts.

Typically, some students became frustrated with each other during a session and shouted out in frustration, maybe expecting that to resolve their conflict. I countered this by telling them to talk with the players involved and try to reach an agreement. Most often, this was enough to settle the conflict, and I seldom had to moderate through restrictions.

Completing the Tasks

During our first sessions of play, it became evident that the assignment sets took longer to complete than I had anticipated. So one of the first adjustments I made was to let students progress through a level at their own speed. Once they finished an assignment, they would contact me and then receive feedback, a reward, and the next assignment.

Although the text material presented in the lobby summed up the formal content that the game was based on, it was not by reading this that the students learned the content.

Students learned while they were playing, through reflection and dialogue with each other and me. As an example, one student built enormous walls around his house (**Figure 11.7**). I asked him whether he thought this was a realistic structure, given the life conditions of a tribe. After an exchange of questions and answers about "what the tribe spent most of their time doing" and "how much time do you think it would take a tribe to build a wall like this," the obvious answer was:

They probably didn't have enough time to build something like this.

Figure 11.7
A settlement with walls—a starting point for student reflection.

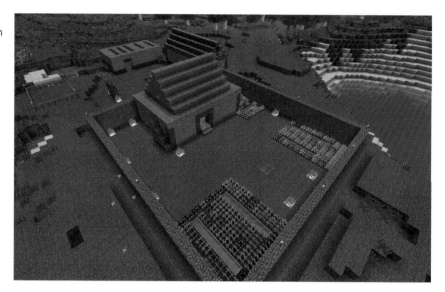

Through this experience of gameplay, reflection, and dialogue, the students acquired knowledge through a first-person experience. Success was realized in how they took on the game premises and how they accepted playing with certain restrictions.

After the first sessions, it also became clear that I needed to be present both in game and in the physical room. Many of the meaningful dialogues came from discussions about how they were building or crafting. The first of these conversations came when I observed students building log cabins that were far too civilized (**Figure 11.8**). Here I had to challenge them to consciously make a primitive design, based on the knowledge they had gained while in the lobby.

Some students responded to these conversations by adjusting their buildings, but others would keep playing, not bothering to make any changes. When they finished their assignment, they received rewards according to how well they had completed the assignments. The challenge for me was to give rewards that actually had value in their gameplay.

Figure 11.8
This design was
too advanced.
Creative students
found it hard
to deliberately
build in a primi-
tive style.

As with many Minecraft projects that have to fit in a schedule, time was not an abundant resource. I had planned for each session a phase in which I would reflect on the gameplay, summarize, and collect feedback. However, I abandoned this plan because I did not want to disrupt the flow and intensity of what was happening in game. Instead, I resorted to reflecting one to one and in groups while they were playing, saving the most important points for the introduction of the next session.

Reflection and Assessment

The most important learning objectives for my students during this course were communication and collaboration. Students were challenged as a group to work on assignments, and this required a high degree of communication and teamwork. I did not do anything to facilitate this process, and I hoped that this would take place while they were playing, but I had not foreseen that students would take the initiative to plan their game carefully outside the classroom sessions.

For many of these students it took a lot of energy to face their peers, discuss, and reflect together. But in the context of a game, this type of dialogue became easier. The reason might be that the game represents a foreseeable system of input and output that can be managed and controlled. Many of my students have a hard time being in a social context that is unforeseeable and irregular. But when the game context becomes the common frame of reference, social interaction is simplified, since it gives a structure to the content of the conversation. Given this reassurance, students have a safe base from which to contribute their thoughts and opinions (**Figure 11.9**), knowing that they are experts when it comes to playing.

Figure 11.9
Students working together on their first shelter.

I met one of my students about a year after playing Civcraft and he keenly recalled our sessions, saying:

That game we played was fun; are you still playing it?

During his involvement in the project, the same student headed up the planning meetings with his tribe during lunch breaks.

A student so eagerly recalling his sessions of play makes it clear for me what learning in games does from a student perspective. It creates an experience that is memorable. It's rich in social exchanges, interactions, failure, and success, and it's all tied together in a narrative in which the players themselves become the main characters.

The "engines" behind the learning were all in the playful approach: competition, challenge, creation, and exploration—to name a few. When these students entered the workshop, their mindset was to have fun, and fortunately, we had the luxury of not being obligated by a certain curriculum. In this setting, it is my perception that students have acquired a fair amount of knowledge through playing in this informal environment. I have gathered this from seeing the way they played, from conversations, and by observing the structures they built.

With this in mind I still see the need to create lesson plans to facilitate pre-game planning and research and post-game reflection. In other words, bringing experiences and thoughts from the game (the informal setting) into the formal setting (the learning space). For students, it means that they would reflect on their play, using their experiences in play as a resource when constructing formal knowledge. Letting students conduct more research before playing and letting them plan some assignments before logging in would help them construct that formal knowledge. Letting them blog on their progress and recording their reflections through text, screenshots, and video would let them process the gameplay.

Playing Civcraft is an ideal way of bringing history to life, but it can also be seen as an interdisciplinary platform to work with content from subjects such as math, civics, and language arts. With this approach, teachers can open various subjects using the story of a civilization as the connecting thread.

Project Future

During my work with Civcraft, I have recognized several designs that are worth developing. At the time of this writing, preliminary plans have been discussed with the National Museum to bring Minecraft into their school service, based on the Civcraft approach.

I think the game in its current form can be seen as a functional "first playable." Many parts of the game need rethinking and testing before an accessible, flexible, and user-friendly design emerges. A consideration when designing any Minecraft world for a learning context is to keep it open-ended. Many teachers take a map as a starting point and adapt it to suit their purposes and meet the needs of their students. I think a remake of the Civcraft lobby with this in mind for each implementation would change much of the overall design.

A final thought for future development is to explore the use of mods in the game. Several mods are available that support specific content in the Bronze Age and Middle Ages, and now that MinecraftEdu can be loaded with mods with ease, many new possibilities open up.

Resources

Here are some resouces for a better understanding of this project:

- Introducing Civcraft (text and screenshots)—http://gamebased .tumblr.com/post/29499663272/introducing-minecraft-civilization-civcraft-a
- Introduction to Civcraft (video with gameplay footage)—http:// gamebased.tumblr.com/post/31390755495/introduction-to-civcraft-with-some-footage-from
- Civcraft Round 2 (video)—http://gamebased.tumblr.com/post/ 33790349849/civcraft-round-2-classroom-walkthrough-and-game
- Civcraft Round 3 and 4 (video)—http://gamebased.tumblr.com/ post/41944150002/heres-some-footage-from-civcraft-round-3-4

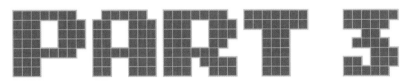

PART 3

Minecraft—Where Next?

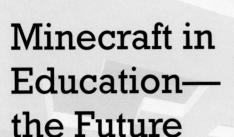

Minecraft in Education— the Future

It's a very hard thing to predict the future, especially anything to do with technology or education. As you have seen over the last several chapters, the ways Minecraft can be used in education are vast if not unlimited. If you look at the broader picture, we haven't even scratched the surface of its applications.

Where Minecraft will be in the realms of education in the future is hard to see. The company behind MinecraftEdu is in the process of releasing Kerbal Space Program Edu, which deals with sending aliens (the Kerbals) to space and back. The game is based heavily on authentic orbital mechanics, aerodynamics, forces, and rocket science! Imagine the fun and engagement that students can have learning those very complex aspects of science.

One reason Minecraft has worked so well in education is that it wasn't made for education. The problem with a lot of "educational" games is that sometimes the educational aspect comes first, whereas factors like creativity should probably take higher priority.

The fact that there is a lively and passionate group of people using Minecraft (and not just in education) means that more and more exciting things will occur over time.

Two trends that have occurred over the last two years will, I think, appear more frequently in Minecraft's educational uses in the near future:

- Computer programming in Minecraft
- Minecraft interacting in the real world and vice versa

Computer Programming in Minecraft

Children are increasingly aware of mods in Minecraft. Children have come to realize that mods are made by "normal" people around the world, and given time and patience, they might be able to learn and create their own mods.

A major push has started for schools to teach coding, and programs such as Scratch have become very popular in classrooms in recent years. The simple drag-and-drop blocks in Scratch give students a way to ease into the complex world of computer programming. Scratch has been used to tell stories, create games, and to show students' learning in numerous subjects. I only recently got into Scratch and offered it during a game-making after school club. I was aware of Scratch for many years but just didn't see the "hook." But it is relevant to our students. I spent weeks in our club teaching how to make a simple maze game, and the modifications and variations of the classic maze game that the students came up with were fascinating.

With the immense popularity of Minecraft, using it to capture students' interest in programmming just makes sense.

Progamming within Minecraft is nothing new, and there have been mods to let people program within Minecraft for a couple of years now.

ComputerCraft (www.computercraft.info) is one such mod. It brings a DOS-type computer block into the game, and you can run commands. It also has turtle blocks into which you can type commands to make the turtle move around the Minecraft world. You can even program the turtles to do all the manual labor of digging in Minecraft. ComputerCraft has been used to create mini-games within Minecraft, like Connect 4 and checkers. You only need to search YouTube to see the amazing projects people have accomplished using Computercraft.

ScriptCraft (www.scriptcraftjs.org) is another example of a mod that enables programming within Minecraft. With ScriptCraft you type the code directly into the chat area of Minecraft, as compared to using computer blocks in ComputerCraft. Again, ScriptCraft exists to enable users to program add-ons or to make mini-games in their Minecraft worlds.

I mention these two mods because they both give a taste of a programming language: Lua for ComputerCraft, and Javascript for ScriptCraft. Bringing some basic programming to students, especially younger students, can be very daunting for a classroom teacher to consider. Of course some students and teachers can jump onboard with these mods without an issue, but there hasn't been a programming environment for Minecraft that has angled itself nicely for education. Until LearnToMod came along.

LearnToMod

At the time of this writing, LearnToMod is *the* up-and-coming tool for children to learn programming. When it's released in October 2014, we could see LearnToMod playing a pivotal part in engaging students in programming. I was fortunate enough to get an early look at what all the hype is about.

It looks like LearnToMod will charge a monthly rental fee for their servers, and each server will allow up to four players (larger servers can be requested). An initial one-time payment gives you a server that you can run your programmed mods in, a web browser-based modding studio to program your mods, and learning materials (the price at the time of this writing is $10 a month for server rental if you purchase the $30 pre-order of Learn2Mod). It's yet to be seen whether they will bundle licenses for classroom editions and prices may change after the initial pre-order period.

The major aspect of LearntoMod that caught my eye and the eyes of many educators around the world is the Scratch-like programming interface that you create your programs in. They are using Blockly (which is actually a Google project) for the interface, but you have the choice to program directly in JavaScript too. It's the drag-and-drop aspect of Blockly, which has a less steep learning curve, that might make LearnToMod the go-to tool to engage students in programming using Minecraft.

Setting Up and Getting Started

I'm not going to run through every step in using LearnToMod, but I will go through my initial interactions with this new tool.

I was given a web address for my own modding studio (where you do all your coding). From there, I received an IP address to input into my local Minecraft installation, which gained me entry into my LearnTo-Mod server so I could see the result of my programs. The first time I accessed the world, I typed a command into the text area of Minecraft, telling Minecraft to connect back to the LearnToMod modding studio. I did not need to do so again.

In my LearnToMod modding studio, there is a home page (**Figure 12.1**) where I can go through numerous tasks, from starting my first program to more complex coding to earning achievement badges (**Figure 12.2**).

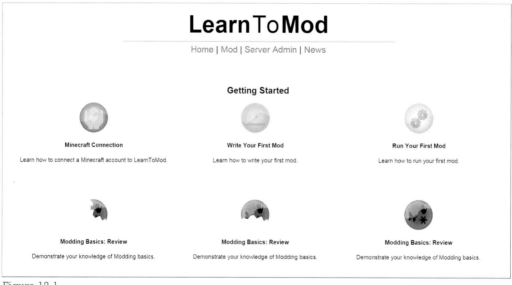

Figure 12.1
If you start from the start and go through each menu, you will start learning more and earning badges as you go.

Figure 12.2
When I success-
fully connected
my Minecraft
account to Learn-
ToMod, I got
my first achieve-
ment badge.

Once connected, you can start building your mods—starting from the start is a good first step (**Figure 12.3**).

Figure 12.3
Every adventure
in coding needs
a nice introduc-
tory stage.

After deciding to use the Getting Started menu option, I got a very simple set of instructions to make my first event happen in Minecraft (**Figure 12.4**). If you have used Scratch before, you can see the similarities.

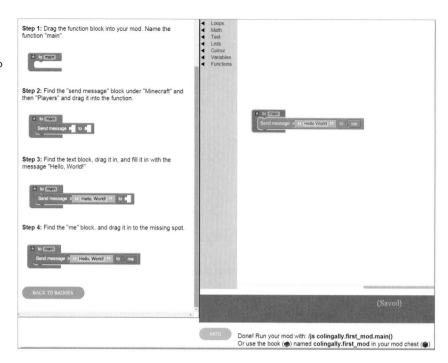

Figure 12.4
The main interface is not that overwhelming to a novice coder.

After finding and dragging all my blocks into the main coding window, I pressed the MOD button at the bottom of the page, which gives me the command to type into the Minecraft chat area (**Figure 12.5**), or I can open it from my LearnToMod Command chest (you won't find these in vanilla Minecraft) in my inventory in-game.

Figure 12.5
I have pasted the command in the chat area, and all I need to do now is press Enter.

```
You are now connected. You may run /connected to verify.
colingally ran a command: /connect
 5f507c8da260fe90f45ce3d3e6041d2eef719146
Mod loaded (first_mod)

/js colingally.first_mod.main()
```

So with my basic knowledge of coding, I think that I should receive a message saying "Hello World" in the Minecraft chat messages (**Figure 12.6**). That's if I arranged my code properly.

It's worth noting that back in the modding studio you can switch between the Blockly interface and JavaScript. Seeing the relationship between the raw code and the block layout is a great idea (**Figure 12.7**).

Figure 12.6
Hurray! I've
coded something
in Minecraft!
Simple, I know,
but it's a start.

Figure 12.7
Memories of my
software devel-
opment days
back in college...

Programming Drones

I will go through another basic introductory program that LearnToMod supplies to get you thinking about what you could do with coding in Minecraft. The creators of LearnToMod use the word *drone* to describe an invisible "cursor" in a Minecraft world. You can basically program a drone where to go and what actions to perform. The program they instruct you to perform will have the drone moving in one direction, placing a brick block as it goes (**Figure 12.8**).

Reading the program blocks from top to bottom: The program creates a drone, which then places a brick block. It moves up one block space and places another brick block; it moves up one more block space and places another brick block.

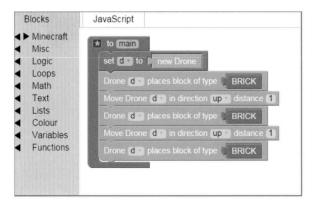

Figure 12.8
The colored
blocks help dif-
ferentiate which
menus (on the
left) the blocks
have come from.

By pressing the MOD button at the bottom of my modding studio, I get the code I need to execute the program. This time, though, I will just grab the mod from my mod chest in-game (**Figures 12.9** and **12.10**).

Figure 12.9
I take this book from my chest, put it in my hand, and right-click to see if my progam works.

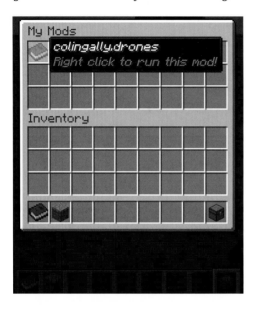

Figure 12.10
Three brick blocks appeared vertically in front of me when I right-clicked the grassy area.

A quick look back into the modding studio lets you see what the JavaScript for this program looks like (**Figure 12.11**).

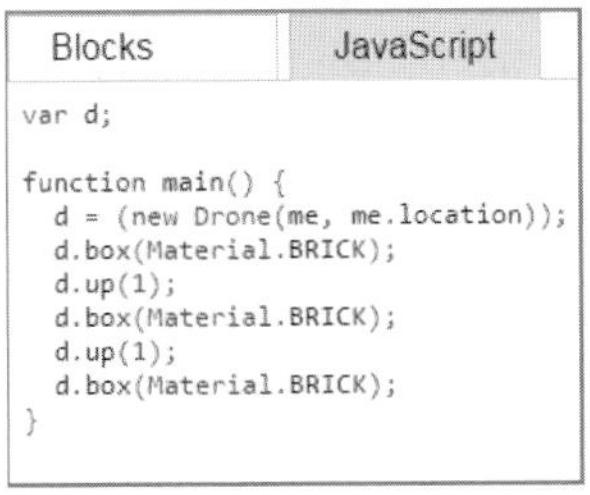

```
  Blocks          JavaScript

var d;

function main() {
    d = (new Drone(me, me.location));
    d.box(Material.BRICK);
    d.up(1);
    d.box(Material.BRICK);
    d.up(1);
    d.box(Material.BRICK);
}
```

Figure 12.11
A little bit more complex than the previous program, but you can see some common syntaxes.

After completing this simple drone program, I began to imagine the different ways drones could be used—from building simple structures to designing complex patterns.

Minecraft and the Real World

It all started with Lego releasing Minecraft sets (I bet they wish they'd thought of creating Minecraft), and it has gone on from there. The crossover of Minecraft and the real world has taken on many forms, and with each month there is another example of somebody somewhere either taking something from Minecraft and dropping it in the real world or taking something from the real world and transforming it in Minecraft. The fascination with this meshing of realities has inspired people worldwide to do some amazing things.

An Opera Performed Within Minecraft

How does performing an opera accompanied by scenes in Minecraft work as a performing arts project? Really well, it seems. Virginia Tech University organized a group of high school students to create a virtual set in Minecraft and create an opera around it. It was dubbed Operacraft (http://tinyurl.com/operacraft). The project culminated in two live performances. The score was sung live, and the scenes in Minecraft were acted out on a big screen. This was live-streamed at the time, but unfortunately it seems to be unavailable now. I remember watching the live stream and thinking about how much time the students must have put into the set creations, the timing of the character movements, and the intricacies of the "camera" placement. They even used a mod that moved the characters' mouths in time with the vocals.

Imagine the engagement this provided to a group of high school students, who otherwise would probably shun opera tickets. Are we to look to Minecraft as the common learning ground for areas that students don't show a lot of interest in?

Operacraft is a shining example of Minecraft being a core part of a complex educational project. Without knowing the fine details of it all, I can only imagine that it builds upon skills such as collaboration and communication, rhythm and composition, and storytelling and expression.

Operacraft is an example of the ever-growing trend of Minecraft and the real world working together to create a new form of media.

Denmark Re-created in Minecraft

Simon Kokkendorf and Thorbjørn Nielsen of the Danish Geodata Agency used topographic data and other physical data models of Denmark to create their country in Minecraft (http://tinyurl.com/denmarkMC). They made this world available to everyone to access and modify. This is another example of an organization realizing the engagment of Minecraft and hoping to get more interest in their field.

What was interesting about this project was the media coverage. At first, the media were just enthralled that an entire country had been converted from spatial data into Minecraft. Then, when the inevitable happened and users started "vandalizing" Minecraft Denmark (the world was left open to users to build), the media had to then report on the other side of Minecraft. Debate and discussions about the online behavior of society was a common thread in these debates. My conclusion is that if you give some people room to make bad decisions without consequence and with total anonymity, they will.

But the overall takeaway people had was awe and fascination that an entire country had been re-created in Minecraft from real-world data (**Figures 12.12** and **12.13**).

Figure 12.12
Banegårdsp-
ladsen, as seen
from above in
Minecraft.

Figure 12.13
Banegårdsplad-
sen, as seen in
Google Maps.

Block by Block

Block by Block is a partnership between Mojang (the creators of Minecraft) and the United Nations Human Settlements Programme. Their mission is to get people involved in urban planning around the world, using Minecraft as the main design and planning tool (http:// blockbyblock.org). One of the most recent projects saw a group of people come together in Lima, Peru, to redesign a city park. Minecraft was used to vizualize how the park could be redesigned.

In all the Block by Block projects, people in developing countries use Minecraft to conceptualize ideas and thoughts into a digital reality, and then from the digital reality into real-world reality. The people in these countries may not have had experience with Minecraft, but with its shallow learning curve, people can get into designing and creating in a very short time. Block by Block bridges the divide between Minecraft and the real world to make the world a better place.

These recent projects have one common thread: creations in the Minecraft world crossing over into the physical world, and vice versa. In other words, creativity in Minecraft becomes a real, physical product, and inspiration from the physical world becomes a product in the Minecraft world. It's that interchange of realities that makes the future of Minecraft very exciting.

The fact that people are already realizing this potential is a sign that this overlapping of worlds may evolve a great deal in the near future.

Minecraft and 3D Printing

How can we, as educators, get started blending Minecraft and the real world? 3D printing. With the falling prices of 3D printers and a lot of schools already owning them, 3D printing is becoming very popular as part of the upsurge in design in education.

With the engagement of Minecraft comes the perfect opportunity to embed the concept of creating objects in Minecraft and then making them in the real world. Students can go through an entire design project, learning design skills and the stages of design, being fully aware that their Minecraft creation will exist in the real world when they are finished.

Adam Clark has been involved in many innovative and educational projects in the United Kingdom. I interviewed him in March 2013 to talk about the numerous projects he has been involved with, most notably the creation of a fully immersive 3D representation of the Tate gallery's paintings—an amazing idea to get younger visitors into art galleries and to get museums more engaged with their collections.

Adam Clarke

I am a freelance creator and technologist in the games-based learning sector, delivering and consulting on its uses and application, with special focus on Minecraft in education, arts and cultural interpretation, and engagement using games. I have over 20 years experience running traditional and digital workshops. I run a small studio arts workshop in the north of England.

Adam is always on top of getting the most of Minecraft, so who better to lead us into the journey of 3D printing from Minecraft?

Playing, Making, and Learning in 3D

Minecraft and 3D printing are two technology success stories; both have seen incredible growth in the last few years. One started as an indie game that has become synonymous with creativity, fun, and engagement, and the other as an industrial process that has made its way into homes, garages, and even supermarkets. You can get yourself scanned as an image and 3D printed in an afternoon; it's as easy as having your photograph taken. As we enter these pioneering times, it's no surprise that educators, inventors, and software engineers have given us the tools to transfer the incredible creative building possibilities in Minecraft into 3D printed objects (**Figure 13.1**). For education and public engagement, this is very exciting because it can combine science, technology, design, history, and narrative storytelling through the playful creation of 3D toys, structures, and artifacts. I use 3D printing and Minecraft to inspire and create a curious mindset in which questions, research, and discovery are student-led.

Figure 13.1
Creeper-head
pendant made
in the Print-
craft server.

Making Minecraft Real

3D printing is the additive manufacturing process of making three-dimensional solid objects from a digital file. The printed object is produced by laying down successive layers of material until the entire object is created. Each layer of material can be imagined as a horizontal cross-section of the eventual object, each slice being only paper thin.

Each digital file has to be prepared with a special 3D modeling print program. This software slices the 3D digital source file into horizontal slices and sends that information to the printer. The printer then extrudes a thin layer of thermal plastic in the shape of the layer.

Lots of different types of 3D printing exist, from selective laser sintering to stereolithography. We'll be focusing on the personal and hobby printing process called fused filament fabrication. This technology uses a spool of thermal plastic filament that is unwound and extruded through a heated nozzle. The extrusion nozzles lay down the thermoplastic material on a build platform. The nozzles move in x and y positions, drawing out the thin layer of the design, while the build platform moves down after each layer is completed to accommodate the next layer. The x-, y-, z-axis can be clearly observed and understood and is a great way to understand and teach about 3D space. Each axis uses computer-controlled stepper motors in the x y via a toothed belt and in the z by a leadscrew.

Every 3D printed object starts with a virtual design. These virtual designs are often created using a computer-aided design (CAD) 3D modeling program. You can even use a scanner to scan a real object and use that digital file as a source for the 3D printer software to slice.

So why use Minecraft? Minecraft is already being used to visualize 3D spaces, forms, and ideas, and it's a creative 3D language that players and educators are playing and learning with already. So why not use Minecraft as a design tool and as an introduction to CAD and 3D printing?

Minecraft 3D Printing

How do you get started? First build something awesome in Minecraft, but be warned that the blocks you want to print must be touching each others' faces (**Figure 13.2**). Blocks on edges will simply fall apart or fail when printed.

Figure 13.2
Place blocks
face to face. The
blocks on the
left will fall apart
when printed;
the blocks on
the right will
print well.

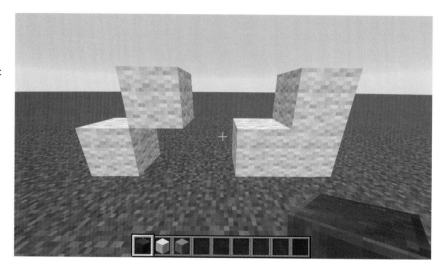

Think about what you are going to design and how it's going to be printed. For example, the model of Big Ben in **Figure 13.3** will look amazing when printed in Full Color Sandstone by Shapeways, a 3D printing service; because of the industrial 3D printing process, complex shapes are easily printed. But when printing with a desktop fused filament 3D printer, you will need to incorporate supports for overhanging or bridging gaps, as the plastic print material needs to stick and solidify to a flat surface. Because of this I often don't include overhangs or bridging gaps in my designs.

Without printing a supporting material, bridges and overhangs will just be printed into thin air, and the result will be a spool of plastic spaghetti. I often design things lying on their backs and use single-colored Minecraft blocks to emulate the single-colored plastic filament (**Figure 13.4**). When my students design in Minecraft, I encourage them to think about shape, depth, shadow, and extrusions. Building one layer at a time from the ground up can also help because the printer will print one layer of plastic at a time; this can stop any hidden holes in your students' work.

Figure 13.3
Big Ben print by
Shapeways in Full
Color Sandstone.

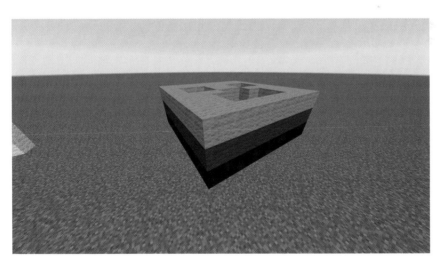

Figure 13.4
Creeper face in
colored layers.

Exporting Minecraft Map Elements

There are two main tools that I use to convert and then export Minecraft map elements into printable 3D files. Each of these tools can produce two types of files: a commercial print file for printing at Shapeways and a file you can print using your own desktop 3D printer.

Mineways

The first tool is Mineways, a free, open-source program for exporting Minecraft models for 3D printing or rendering. It's downloadable for Mac, Windows, and Linux—with detailed installation instructions on the website, as well as documentation on how to use it. I'll give a brief outline of how I use it for printing in the studio and classroom, and even for sending away to a commercial printer.

When you first open Mineways, you might get a warning message (**Figure 13.5**) explaining that Mineways could not "find your Minecraft world saves directory."

Figure 13.5
Mineways warn-
ing message.

You'll have to find it manually. This is not a big problem. In the Mineways application window, choose File > Open to see a list of the worlds that are saved on the computer you are using. If you need to search manually for your worlds, choose File > Open World to search for your Minecraft world. When searching for it manually, you will need to find the level.dat file that lives inside your Minecraft saved world folder. This level.dat file contains all the block positions and data in your Minecraft world. To navigate to it on a Mac, go to Users/YourUserName/Library/Application Support/minecraft/saves/TheWorldFolder/level.dat.

On a computer running Windows, go to C:\Users\YourUserName\AppData\Roaming\.minecraft\saves\TheWorldFolder\level.dat.

Once your world is loaded into the window, you can drag the map to navigate around your world (**Figure 13.6**).

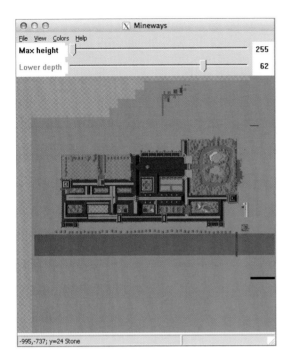

Figure 13.6
Top-down view
of a Minecraft
map in Mineways.

Building initially on a flat world can help when trying to find your work or your students' work. You can zoom in and out with your mouse scroll wheel (**Figure 13.7**). Once you have located the object you want to export, simply right-click and drag a selection box around the object. If some of your visible blocks are outside the selection area, a warning dialog will appear letting you know. You can adjust this by clicking OK and repositioning the box edges by right-clicking and dragging them.

You now have a selected Minecraft object; you can export it for a commercial printer or your own desktop 3D printer.

Full-colored sandstone is perfect for figurines and life-like models. Models are created by printing binder material and colored ink layer by layer into a bed of gypsum-based powder. After printing, the models are finished with a cyanoacrylate (super glue) sealant to ensure durability and vivid colors. The final product is a hard, brittle material that works great for figurines and visual models, but it isn't well suited to functional parts or daily handing. This kind of printing can get a bit expensive because Shapeways sells its products by volume of printed material, so think small, and if you can hollow out your objects, do. Shapeways and other commercial printers use a fine, powdered support material that can be vacuumed and brushed away from the final printed models, so they can print impossible and even interlocking shapes. Your only concerns with a Minecraft print are the thinness of your walls and thin tree trunks that could easily snap in transit.

Figure 13.7
Pink selection box around a Minecraft building.

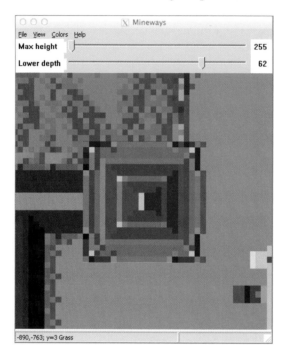

To create a 3D file to send to Shapeways and print in full-colored sandstone, choose File > Export for 3D Printing.

A dialog (**Figure 13.8**) will appear in which you can name the file and navigate to where you want to save the files.

Figure 13.8
Saving your selection for Shapeways.

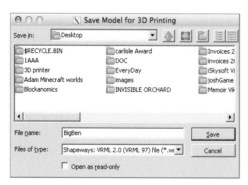

I always make a new folder for each saved file because the export process creates three files during this type of save. Notice the File of Type drop-down menu giving different options—we'll be using the Shapeways: VRML 2.0 option. Click Save to open yet another dialog with what seems to be a dizzying array of options (**Figure 13.9**). Most of the time I just click OK, but you should take a look around the different parameters, especially in the Scale section, and note the Model's Units setting, which is often set to Millimeters.

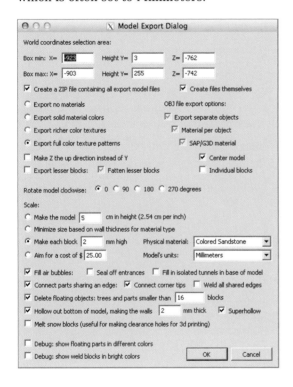

Figure 13.9
Mineways
export dialog.

If you're a Mac user you might get an error message here: Error: no terranExt.png file found.

Simply click OK, and then in the Mineways window choose File > Set Terrain File. A little window will appear. You'll need to navigate and manually find the terranExt.png file—often in the same folder that the Mineways application is located. Once you have manually found the file, go back and follow the export steps.

You'll know you have successfully exported the model when you see the dialog (**Figure 13.10**) with your 3D print statistics in it, showing approximate cost, size, and total blocks.

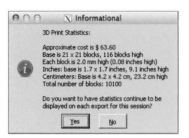

You will see three files that have been exported: a PNG file, a WRL file, and a ZIP file. The ZIP file is a conveniently compressed file containing the PNG and WRL files, ready for uploading to Shapeways.

Open a web browser and navigate to www.shapeways.com. Sign up for a free account and go to My Models.

Click the Upload button, and navigate to and select the ZIP file to start the upload.

Remember that the dimensions are millimeters. Shapeways will process the file, and if all goes well a 3D thumbnail will appear with the different types of material options available.

Choose colored sandstone, and if you can afford it, buy one. If things go wrong, Shapeways will list the errors. Most often it's a mismatch in dimensions, but there is a comprehensive FAQ and a support section. The model is then printed by Shapeways at their 3D print factory and shipped to you in roughly three to four weeks.

Printcraft

The second way I create 3D Minecraft print files is probably the easiest and most fun way I can think of. It's also great for groups and classes to work together. It uses an amazing Minecraft Bukkit plug-in and web service developed by Paul Harter, a self-described digital toolmaker. This method allows you to create 3D models in a Minecraft world and with a click of a redstone button a 3D file is created. You can then download it from the website, and it is ready to print with your own 3D printer in minutes.

Printcraft is very easy to use. There are two Minecraft servers with the ability to capture your creations and turn them into STL files for 3D printing. One server is in Europe (eu1.printcraft.org), and one is in America (us1.printcraft.org).

When you log in to one of the servers, you'll find a number of square glowstone building plots marked out on the ground, and next to each will be a control panel.

Build something inside the plot (**Figure 13.11**). Remember to build from the ground up.

Figure 13.11
Printcraft building plots.

When you are ready, click the Print button on the control panel (**Figure 13.12**). This will send your model off to be processed by the server and will write a web link into the Minecraft chat. Click this link to open the model and launch www.printcraft.org. From the website, you can download a Standard Tessellation Language (STL) file of your model to print yourself. An STL file is a file format native to the stereolithography CAD software. This file format is supported by many software packages. Or you can have it printed by Materialise or Shapeways and sent to you. Make sure your school or institution allows access to the website before your session begins.

Figure 13.12
Printcraft con-
trol panel.

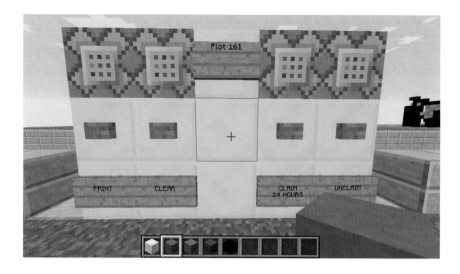

The Clear button will clear all the blocks in the building plot. The Claim button will lock the plot so that other players cannot add or delete blocks. This helps protect your model from griefing. The claim lasts one week, but you can extend it at any time by pressing Claim again. You can unclaim the plot by pressing the Unclaim button. You can add a friend to your plot by typing the /ppadd playername command, and remove them by typing the /ppremove playername command.

This way of making and creating printable 3D files is great fun for a class or group. They can share ideas and even collaborate in a famil-iar Minecraft world, showing off their skills and seeing other people's models. Remember that these are public servers, so the usual Internet safety rules must apply—but because they are creative and educational in nature, they are often free from nasty behavior and usually pretty empty, used mostly by schools and creative individuals.

Using Your Own Printer

There are many types of printers on the market. I chose one that was an affordable entry-level printer. The Flashforge dual extruder uses the same print software as the MakerBot range (**Figure 13.13**).

The range of printers offered can be intimidating, so here are a few pointers to help you buy your first printer.

Figure 13.13
Flashforge
dual extruder.

Find out what software is needed to print. I choose Flashforge because it can use MakerWare and is simple and easy to use.

You need to ask questions: What kinds of thermal filament does it use? Is it too specialized? Where can you get spare parts? What kind of support can you expect from the people who sell it to you?

I bought mine online, and the support has been great: online chat and additional PDF documentation for the printer. Start with a printer that you feel reasonably confident with. I learned along the way, watched many YouTube videos, read online articles, and joined discussion groups.

The Flashforge uses the same print software as the MakerBot range (MakerWare), so I'll use that as an example.

Once you have unboxed the printer, turned it on, set up the spool, and leveled the build plate, you're ready to print. You can plug your printer into your computer or export the file to an SD card and use that to print from.

It took me about three weeks of testing before I was happy with how I leveled the build plate. I made lots of mistakes along the way, but I got to know the software and printer a little more. Hopefully these instructions will help you speed up that process. I received two types of plastic filament spools: ABS and PLA. ABS plastic is high strength, impact and heat resistant, a good electrical insulator, and moisture resistant, and it has a high strength to weight ratio. PLA (polylactic acid) is derived from corn and is biodegradable so it's a little more environmentally friendly. It can often start a cool discussion around chemistry and the molecular bonds of lactic acid. Both filaments have strengths and weaknesses.

I usually print with PLA and generally do not heat my build plate. You can heat the build plate to stop warping of the extruded plastic as it cools. I've had only a few problems with warping. I don't heat the build plate because it can burn curious fingers—the plate is heated to 120 degrees Celsius. I work with children in a busy studio, so I heat only the extrusion nozzles and give clear warnings, instructions, and reminders never to touch the nozzles or the working printer. Each nozzle is heated to 230 degrees Celsius. These temperatures are dangerous, and a good health and safety talk followed by a discussion about how to measure them is always a good idea. I also use 3M ScotchBlue 2090 painter's tape carefully stuck down to the build plate because it helps reduce warping (**Figure 13.14**).

Figure 13.14
Minecraft swords printed on blue painter's tape as a support.

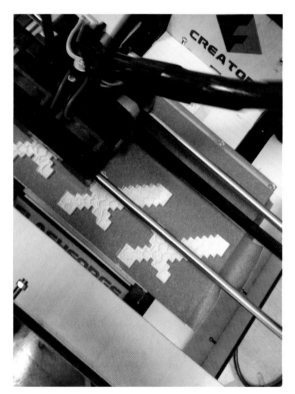

Leveling the build plate regularly is important, and I always start a print session this way.

I use MakerWare software to print my STL file. This is the software that converts a 3D source file into slices that the printer understands. MakerWare has comprehensive support documents available online, so be sure to read them.

The MakerWare interface is very intuitive. You simply use the add (+) button (**Figure 13.15**) to import your STL file into MakerWare.

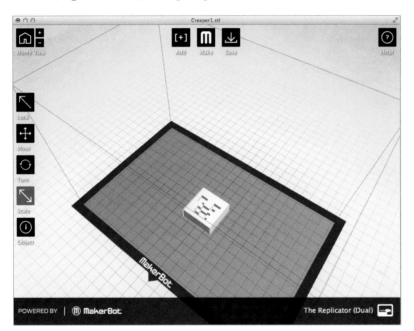

Figure 13.15
A creeper head imported into MakerWare.

Understanding rafts and supports can help you get printing quickly. The MakerWare interface (**Figure 13.16**) gives you the option to print a raft and supports. A raft is a flat area printed on the build plate to support your main print and can help if your prints are not sticking or connecting to the build plate. MakerWare also creates a special wall or curtain to catch the droplets of plastic that will drop from the hot nozzles. The curtains are super lightweight and designed to help you get the best results.

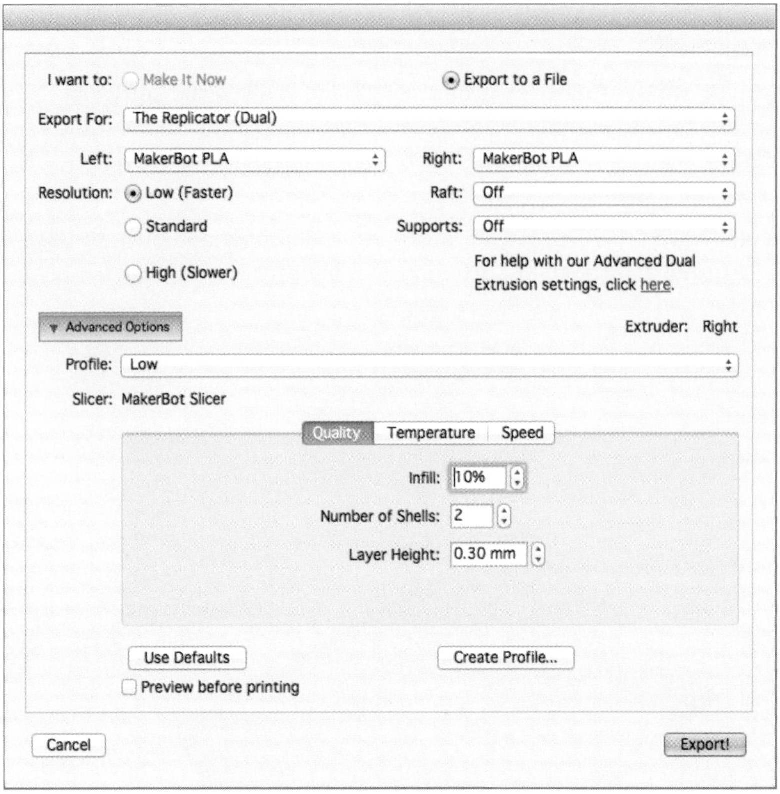

Figure 13.16
MakerWare
export dialog.

Supports are created to support overhangs or bridges during the print process. I suggest investigating these when you feel more confident. There are a range of a water-soluble PVA filaments to create supports that simply wash away after you have printed with them, making excellent support material and another good opportunity for learning about print processes, engineering, and manufacturing.

Try something small for your first print. Good luck!

When Things Go Wrong

Things will go wrong, so don't be surprised when they do—it's part of the process and a great way to learn. Some of my early mistakes were misadjusting the build plate and sending the wrong information to the printer in the first place (**Figure 13.17**). Experiment and have fun. If you're still having trouble weeks later, seek online support and share your experiences with the growing community of makers. I'm sure they've made all the same errors and will be happy to give excellent tips for your future adventures.

Figure 13.17
Printcraft STL house not sticking to the raft.

It's always amazing to see a 3D print slowly forming. I often see my young people gathered around the printer, transfixed, as the plastic extruders build layer upon layer. I also love watching my students' work and designs coming to life.

Creating Mashups

Once you have the hang of 3D printing, you might want to try something a little more experimental. Mashups are the combination of a range of source materials to create something surprising and new. I make 3D mashups with Tinkercad (an online CAD service) and Minecraft STL files. I also download STL files from www.thingverse.com.

For example, I love sticking Minecraft models into Lego (**Figure 13.18**) and making new things from existing shapes and forms. All this is very easy with Tinkercad. It can import STL files that you have created and stick them together in fun and amazing ways. Check it out at https://tinkercad.com. I have a fun tutorial video about Tinkercad in my 101 Ideas for Minecraft Learners series that will help new users get started (www.tinyurl.com/adamytplist).

Figure 13.18
Creeper Lego
mashup.

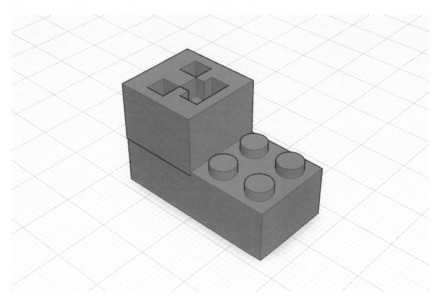

Lesson Ideas

The learning opportunities with 3D printing are endless, but here are a few that I find intriguing:

- Design a chess set and other board game derivatives; for example, Monopoly houses.
- Make some awesome Minecraft dice—creeperface for six!
- Create pyramids, spheres, and so on.
- Try some Lego mashups. Combine your Minecraft creations with STL Lego pieces.
- Build a historical replica; for example, a building, a temple, or a ship.
- Build a blocky alphabet and experiment with font types.
- Create creeper bling and other Minecraft-inspired jewelry. My first project was a creeper keychain.
- Design chests or boxes. This can be great for experimenting with two-piece designs.

Resources

Listed here are programs and tools that can assist with learning and using 3D printing in your projects:

- **MakerBot:** www.makerbot.com

  MakerWare is a program made by MakerBot that allows you to easily prepare 3D models for building. There is extensive online documentation and email support.

- **Tinkercad:** https://tinkercad.com

  Tinkercad is an easy-to-use tool for creating digital designs that are ready to be 3D printed into physical objects. Users are guided through the 3D design process through "lessons," which teach the basics before moving on to more complex modeling techniques. This is a powerful tool that uses WebGl and 3D web standards and is available on the Google Chrome and Mozzlla Firefox web browsers. Tinkercad is an easy-to-use and child-friendly 3D CAD environment. But don't be fooled—you can make some pretty complex things with it.

Tinkercad can export a 3D file, but more amazingly, it can export a Minecraft schematic. Minecraft schematics are selections of a Minecaft world, and you can use a program called MCedit to insert them into your own world. I have made giant robots, space stations, and cityscapes. It's a great way to engage CAD skills and Minecraft in the classroom.

- **MCEdit:** www.mcedit.net

MCEdit is an open-source world editor for Minecraft. It was created to allow players to preserve anything built with several old versions of Minecraft and take them forward into newer versions of the game. It also aims to be forward-compatible with future (or even modified) versions of Minecraft. MCEdit has since been improved with brush tools for laying down blocks in different shapes and importing schematics, and it has a range of filters to change a world in hundreds of ways. When combined with Tinckercad and 3D printing, a whole new world of possibilities will open up.

- **101 ideas for Minecraft Learners:** http://bit.ly/101IdeasMCLearners

- **Mineways:** www.realtimerendering.com/erich/minecraft/public/mineways

Index